Walk VICTORIA

Your guide to over 50 urban and suburban walks

John Crouch

Chickadee Press
Victoria, BC

Disclaimer
The author and publisher have made every attempt to be as accurate as
possible in describing the walks within this book. However, they relinquish
all responsibility for changes that may have occurred to roadways and paths
since the book's date of publication.

National Library of Canada Cataloguing in Publication
Crouch, John, 1941–
   Walk Victoria: your guide to over 50 urban and suburban walks / John Crouch.
ISBN 0-9731913-0-9
   1. Walking—British Columbia—Victoria—Guidebooks. 2. Victoria (B.C.)—
Guidebooks. I. Title.
FC3846.18.C76 2003   917.11'28044   C2003-900558-5
F1089.5.V6C76 2003

Cover and book design: Frances Hunter, Beacon Hill Communications Group
Front cover photograph: James R. Smith
Back cover photographs: John Crouch, James R. Smith
Frontispiece: Garry oaks below Christmas Hill
Maps: Jennifer Pullium Green
Photographs: James R. Smith, Lawrence McLagan and John Crouch

First printing, March, 2003
Second printing, May, 2003
Third printing, July, 2003

Printed by Fotoprint, Victoria, BC

Chickadee Press
303 – 1137 View Street
Victoria, BC Canada
V8V 3L9

For Mia and Daniel

Acknowledgements

The task of creating a book out of the imaginings of the mind is a prodigious one. It usually involves a number of people. Fortunately, I've had a group of friends who have generously contributed their skills and talents to the production of this guidebook and I'd like to thank them.

First on my list is Lorinda Raynor. Not only did Lorinda spend hours typing the text she also accompanied me on many of the walks. Her constant enthusiasm and encouragement kept me focused and on track. Jennifer Pullium Green, whose friendship goes back to the sixties, applied her considerable talents to creating the maps. Frances Hunter did a wonderful job designing the book as well as being a constant source of good advice. Jim Smith and Lawrence McLagan were generous in their contribution of photographs. My close friend Brian Connon proofread along with Louise Wood. Joyce Geisler provided moral and financial support. Thank you all.

I'd like to acknowledge the assistance of the following: Saanich Archives; Oak Bay Archives; Esquimalt Archives; Saanich Parks and CRD Parks.

Contents

The Walks

Victoria, Esquimalt and Oak Bay

Saanich and View Royal

Colwood and Langford

Coastline Route: From James Bay to Cordova Bay

(Each walk is *40 mins. to 1 hr.*)

Why this book was written

In the early nineteen-eighties while visiting family and friends in England I took a hiking tour of the Lake District. I was revisiting mountains and lakes, villages and small towns I had been introduced to as a teenager many years before. In almost every store I went into, be it sporting equipment store, pharmacy, gift shop or bookstore, I found a rack of small books that were walking and hiking guides to the local area. By and large, they weren't pretentious affairs — just a map of the route, a description of the walk or hike and a few photographs or sketches.

These were the first in my collection of hiking and walking guides and sit on my bookshelf alongside more extensive and detailed guides to such places as the Swiss Alps, the Pyrenees, the deserts of the southwest United States and, closer to home, Strathcona Park, the Cascade and Olympic Mountains. It is those early books and my more recent additions that have provided the inspiration and model for the book you're reading now.

I've wanted to write a guidebook to walks in and around Victoria that would concentrate on the basics and would entice people, both visitors and residents, to explore and enjoy some of the many attractive and sometimes less familiar areas of the vicinity. And when I talk about basics I mean a book that focuses on the walk with just a few hints at what a walker might experience in terms of plants, wildlife, geographical and other points of interest. I've written from the perspective of someone who enjoys the experience of his of her body moving through space, especially a space that is pleasing to the senses.

While I have an interest in and a rudimentary knowledge of the natural world, I have refrained from providing detailed information of the flora and fauna of a walk knowing that to do so would be beyond the scope of my competence. For those walkers wishing a more naturalist-oriented guide they must look elsewhere. No, my intention is simple — to provide a vehicle through which people can explore, experience and enjoy, in any positive way they choose, the variety of landscapes that surround us here in Victoria.

How to use this book

Each walk is described in a similar manner. First there is an introduction to the walk which usually gives some historical background to the area or points out something of interest. Occasionally some reference is made to plant and wildlife along with an indication of important geographical features. To help the reader decide at a glance whether a walk is of interest in terms of location, length and what it has to offer I've given brief notes under each of the following headings.

General description Here, in a sentence or two, the walk is described very succinctly. The description can refer to terrain — either urban, park or mixed; the type of trail surface — whether paved, gravel or chip or the kind of plants, trees, wildlife or other significant natural element that can be found.

Location Location refers to the distance from Victoria's downtown to the walk's beginning (given in kilometres) and gives a general indication of its geographical location.

Length The length refers to the amount of time in hours and minutes needed, by the average walker, to complete the walk. I've estimated the average walker will cover one kilometre every 12 minutes. For example a five kilometre walk will take one hour.

Level I've used three words to indicate the level of difficulty of a walk. *Easy* means that the walk is flat or gently rolling and requires an average amount of effort. *Moderate* is used to indicate that a greater effort is required as the walk includes some hills. *Strenuous* usually indicates the need to be physically fit and capable of climbing some very steep inclines.

Special attractions This section is used to highlight some of the more interesting features of the walk which could include a view or views, a distinctive natural element or simply a nice place to eat and drink.

How to get there Here directions are given from downtown Victoria to each of the walk's trailhead or starting point by car. A good city road map would be a useful addition in finding a walk's location. Most large grocery and drug stores carry such maps. When possible I've also given bus information. (BC Transit publishes a *Rider's Guide* available on buses and in many stores.)

The walk The final section is the walk itself. I've tried to describe the walks as simply and clearly as possible. I've made little or no attempt to direct the walker to "do" or "see" certain things relying rather on the walker's own sense of what is important and attractive enough for them to do or see. I do however, sometimes suggest what I consider to be good view points, picnic sites or places to eat and drink.

It's a wise practise to consult the accompanying route map while on the walk, matching what is written in the description with what is seen on the map.

Footwear For all the walks included in this book a good pair of walking shoes or low-cut hiking boots is all that is required.

About your dog Having your dog along for a walk is what many consider to be the perfect companion. However, some of the walks described in this book go through nature and wildlife sanctuaries where dogs are not allowed. Also, some beaches and parks only permit dogs during certain times of the year. Just be aware of these restrictions when deciding whether or not to take Rover. •

MAP LEGEND

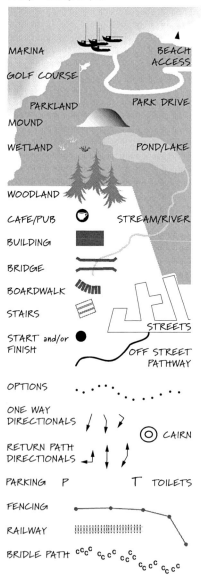

MARINA

BEACH ACCESS

GOLF COURSE

PARKLAND

PARK DRIVE

MOUND

WETLAND

POND/LAKE

WOODLAND

CAFE/PUB

STREAM/RIVER

BUILDING

BRIDGE

BOARDWALK

STAIRS

STREETS

START and/or FINISH

OFF STREET PATHWAY

OPTIONS

ONE WAY DIRECTIONALS

RETURN PATH DIRECTIONALS

CAIRN

PARKING   P

T   TOILETS

FENCING

RAILWAY

BRIDLE PATH

Victoria, Esquimalt and Oak Bay

1 BOWKER CREEK PARK TO WILLOWS BEACH

Bowker Creek has an interesting history. In the 1850s the creek was known locally as Tod's Stream because it passed through the 160-hectare farm of John Tod, an early settler. After his death in 1882 it took the name of Tod's son-in-law John Bowker and became known as Bowker Creek. Early maps of Oak Bay refer to the creek as the Thames River and municipal documents of 1912 make reference to a Thames Valley suggesting that the creek might have been a more substantial body of water than today.

Surprisingly, where the creek met the ocean it flowed through a sizeable ravine which was once used as a garbage dump. In the late 1970's part of the Oak Bay portion of the creek was trans-formed into a park with a railed walkway on its banks. Though running for less than half a kilo-metre, the walkway is one of Oak Bay's most picturesque and tran-quil parks.

The creek has its source in the Gordon Head area close to Feltham Road. The creek winds its way through open areas and culverts into the Shelbourne Street district before emptying into Oak Bay's waterfront.

General description
An out-and-back walk along the tree lined banks of Bowker Creek to the sandy shores of Willows Beach.

Location
About four kilometres from down-town Victoria in the municipality of Oak Bay.

Length 1 – 1.5 hours out-and-back

Level Easy

Special attractions

Tree-lined walkway along a meandering creek; sandy beach with a summer tea house; Willows Beach and Park; the ancient site of a First Nations settlement; oldest house west of the Great Lakes.

How to get there

Take Fort Street out of town. Pass the junction of Oak Bay Avenue, Richmond and Foul Bay Roads. Turn right at the first traffic light after Foul Bay Road (Fort Street is now Cadboro Bay Road) onto Bee Street. Pass the Oak Bay Recreation Centre on the left and turn left on Goldsmith — a deadend street. Park in the parking lot in front of the outdoor track. *(Bus #11 Uplands.)*

THE WALK From the parking lot walk to the left of the **Jack Wallace Memorial Track** crossing a concrete bridge over Bowker Creek. Turn right and walk the 100 metres paralleling the creek to a short flight of steps to the creek waterway. Pass the first bridge and cross the second bridge just before the path meets **Hampshire Road**. Cross the road and follow the waterway path another 50 metres to Monterey Avenue. As you cross Monterey turn left and then right in front of the **Oak Bay Fire Hall** and **Police Station** and continue into **Freeman's Park**. (When the Fire Hall was being built in the 1930s, a large midden was unearthed along with a number of First Nations' artifacts both of which suggested it was the site of a settlement.)

Walk to the right of the **Jack Groves Fieldhouse** exiting the park on Montieth Street. Turn left here walking to and turning right on Cranmore Road. At the junction of **Cranmore** and **Beach Drive** cross Beach and turn left walking 50 metres to an access lane (unmarked) going down to the right. Follow this lane and either walk to the beach and turn left to walk along the sand to **Willows Beach** or turn left on the last roadway before the beach access (Bowker Place) turning first right and then left on the path leading to Willows Beach. On a clear day there are good views of Discovery Island, the San Juan Islands and Mount Baker in the distance.

To walk back. **OPTION ONE** Take the tree-lined path on the carpark side (Dalhousie Street) of Willows Park to Beach Drive. Turn left on

2

Beach walking to its junction with Cranmore. Retrace the walk from Cranmore. **OPTION TWO**: Walk along Willows Beach on Esplanade to **Estevan Avenue**. Turn left on Estevan and walk three blocks to **Heron Street**. Turn right on Heron and walk 40 odd metres to notice a white house behind a white picket fence on the opposite side of the road. The house is number 2564. It's **John Tod's original farm house** which he built in 1851 and is reputedly the oldest house west of the Great Lakes. As you'll see, the house and garden are still in great shape.

After viewing the house return back to Estevan and, crossing the road, continue along Heron. Heron swings sharp left and left again to become **Lincoln Road**. It is at this second corner that you'll notice a narrow paved lane passing between two houses leading to Beach Drive. Take this lane turning right on Beach. Walk back to Cranmore and retrace the walk back to its beginning. •

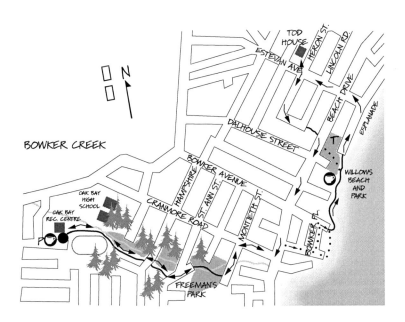

2 BRIGHTON AVENUE

Straddling the municipalities of Victoria and Oak Bay, Brighton Avenue runs parallel to Oak Bay Avenue from Richmond Road to St. David Street.

Historically, the land through which Brighton passes was known as Gonzales Farm — a huge piece of land owned by Joseph Despard Pemberton, the province's first surveyor-general. Gonzales Farm stretched from Rockland Avenue to the Oak Bay waterfront and covered almost 500 hectares of land. To encourage the development of Oak Bay Pemberton constructed Oak Bay Avenue and around 1890 presented it to the city. A year later the Victoria tramway system

JOHN CROUCH

Stairway to Brighton Avenue

extended its Fort Street line down the avenue to the waters of Oak Bay.

During the following few years this tram line, along with enterprising real estate developers, transformed Oak Bay from a farming and summer camping area into a suburb from which people could commute to the city.

Today, Oak Bay is a fully mature municipality and Brighton Avenue, characterized by its intermittent connecting walkways, runs through its heart.

General description
A loop walk through some of Oak Bay's most interesting streets.

Location
Walk starts about two and half

kilometres from downtown on the Victoria — Oak Bay border.

Length 1 hour

Level Easy (with some stairs)

Special attractions
Interconnecting pathways with occasional stairways. Examples of arts and crafts architecture. Tree-lined streets especially horse-chestnut. Bakery and café at McNeill and Roslyn.

How to get there
From downtown take Fort Street going east. At the four-way junction of Fort Street, Pandora and Oak Bay Avenues, turn right onto Oak Bay Avenue. About half a kilometre and at the first traffic light turn right onto Richmond Avenue. Brighton Avenue is the first street on the left. Parking is available on Richmond. *(Bus #2 Oak Bay.)*

THE WALK From **Richmond Avenue** walk four hundred metres down **Brighton Avenue**. This quiet residential street briefly terminates just after **Redfern Street**. Follow the short path that goes between **Brighton Crescent** and **Amphion Street** and connects with the 1000 block of Brighton Avenue.

Cross **Foul Bay Road** walking up the paved driveway to pass through a metal pedestrian barrier and onto a gravel path to the continuation of Brighton. Cross **Victoria Avenue** and, ignoring the "no exit" sign, walk up a slight incline to a narrow gravel path through a grove of Garry oaks. Cross the top of the unsigned **Roslyn Road** to the continu-

ation of the gravel path and down a flight of stone steps to **Hampshire Road**. Cross Hampshire and continue along a stretch of Brighton that is flanked on both sides by magnificent, large horse-chestnut trees.

Follow Brighton as it crosses **Monterey Avenue, Oliver, St. Patrick and St. David Streets**. Across St. David ignore the "no-exit" sign and walk along a narrow uneven lane for 40 metres before descending down a rough trail to meet and cross Transit Road. Bear right taking **St. Denis Street** to **Windsor Road** and **Windsor Park**. Turn right on Windsor and cross the park by the path that passes to the right of the pavilion. Turn right again on Currie Road walking to and turning left on **Transit Road**.

At the next intersection turn right on **McNeill Avenue** walking six blocks to Roslyn. Here there's an opportunity to pause at the **Demitasse Café** before turning right at the next block on Victoria. Walk the two long blocks along the silver birch-lined Victoria Avenue back to Brighton. Turn left on Brighton retracing the route back to Richmond. ●

Springtime in Oak Bay

3 CATTLE POINT TO OAK BAY MARINA

Cattle Point is the shoreline of the 31.25-hectares Uplands Park. This park was originally set aside for recreational use as long ago as 1912 when it was part of the grand subdivision known as Uplands. The municipality of Oak Bay took over the land in 1946 intending to keep it in as natural a state as possible. Uplands Park has a wide variety of plant life including an extensive Garry oak forest. The display board at Cattle Point features photographs and names of the most abundant plants found in the park. The point itself offers opportunities for bird watching especially oystercatchers and the ever-present harlequin ducks.

Cattle Point also marks the entrance to Oak Bay's exclusive neighbourhood of Uplands. This was once part of the Hudson's

JAMES. R. SMITH

Sailing off Cattle Point

Bay Company's Uplands Farm which was bought and divided up into roughly one-acre lots in the early 1900s. Houses in the area had to have a minimum price of $5,000.00 and no multi-family or commercial buildings were allowed.

The long, sandy Willows Beach, 100 or so metres to the south of the Point, is the ancient site of an extinct Songhees First Nation settlement named Sitcha-math. Archaeological evidence suggests that the village was occupied for about 2500 years until the early 1900s. The inter-pretive board by the children's play area graphically depicts what the settlement might have looked like and describes the burial prac-tices and other aspects of the Songhees' history and culture.

General description
A very pleasant and scenic walk along the Oak Bay waterfront.

Location
Eight kilometres from downtown Victoria in the municipality of Oak Bay.

Length 1 hour round trip.

Level Easy

Special attractions
Cattle Point — tidal flats, rocky outcrops, picnic tables, boat ramp, bird watching, ocean and island views.

Uplands Park — Garry oak forest, secluded glades and a profuse dis-play of wildflowers in spring.

Willows Beach — sandy beach, shallow water, children's play area, Willows Park, Kinsmen tearoom, toi-lets, mountain and ocean views.

Glenlyon-Norfolk School — originally designed, built and lived in by the architect F. M. Rattenbury.

Oak Bay Marina — cafe, gift shop, restaurant, yacht club, break-water.

How to get there
From downtown go north on Blanshard turning right onto Fort Street which is one-way for two kilo-metres. Follow Fort Street until it intersects Foul Bay Road. Fort Street now becomes Cadboro Bay Road. Continue along Cadboro Bay Road for two kilometres turning right at a traffic light at the intersection of Lansdowne Road. Descend Lansdowne Road to the water and turn right along Beach Drive. Half a kilometre on the left is Cattle Point. (Bus #11 UVic.)

THE WALK   From the Point's central carpark walk back along the entrance road (west) for 50 metres. Take the path to the left which leads to a flight of stairs down to **Willows Beach**. At the bottom of the stairs take the sidewalk **(Esplanade)** along the beach or walk on the beach. Esplanade ends at the entrance to Willows Park however, and the sidewalk becomes a walkway before ending at **Bowker Avenue**.

Take Bowker until it intersects Beach Drive. Turn left here and walk south along Beach Drive. Just past the **Glenlyon-Norfolk School** (famous as being the home of the brilliant but troubled architect Francis Rattenbury), the sidewalk hugs the seawalk until the grassy area of **Queens' Park** and the entrance to **Oak Bay Marina**. The marina's cafe and restaurant are great places to pause and refresh. A path circles the marina parking lot which offers views of Mary Tod Island and Emily Islet.

Retrace the walk to Bowker Avenue at which point you can either go back to Cattle Point via Willows Beach or follow Beach Drive to Cattle Point. For a slightly longer walk, after the marina, continue south along Beach Drive up a short hill, past the Oak Bay Beach Hotel and on through the Victoria Golf Course. This golf course is exceptionally scenic with the links going down to the shoreline. This will add another two kilometres to the walk.

Across from Cattle Point is **Uplands Park** itself. I have not described this as a walk because the paths are not organized or signed. I say this not to deter walking there, on the contrary, it's a very pleasant place to walk, but to indicate it's a place to explore rather than have a guided walk. The display board at Cattle Point has a map of the park with some trails marked. •

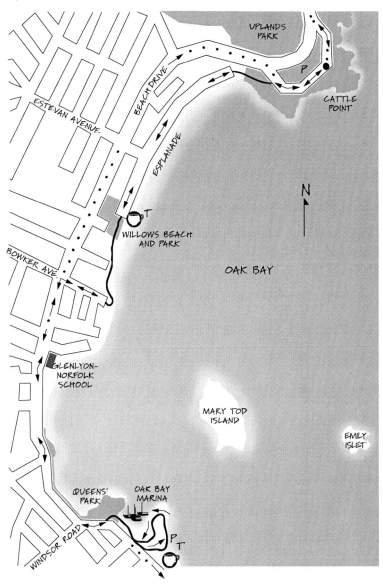

UPLANDS
PARK

BEACH DRIVE

ESTEVAN AVENUE

P

CATTLE
POINT

ESPLANADE

N

T

WILLOWS BEACH
AND PARK

OAK BAY

BOWKER AVE.

GLENLYON-
NORFOLK
SCHOOL

MARY TOD
ISLAND

EMILY
ISLET

QUEENS'
PARK

OAK BAY
MARINA

WINDSOR ROAD

P
T

4 THE GALLOPING GOOSE REGIONAL TRAIL

It's rather appropriate that the Galloping Goose Regional Trail (The Goose) has its start at the Via Rail train station on the Johnson Street bridge. The railroad lines the trail crosses are a visual link with the Goose's own railroad history.

The Galloping Goose was the name given to an ungainly gas-powered rail car that noisily transported people and mail twice daily between Victoria and the western community of Sooke. The car had a short life making its daily runs however and after only nine years of service between 1922 and 1930, the Canadian National Railway discontinued the route.

Since the trail's dedication in 1989, the Capital Regional District has over the past decade transformed the abandoned rail bed into the 57 kilometre linear trail of today.

The section described below is a very small portion of this scenic and multi-use trail.

General description
An out-and-back walk along the mostly paved first section of the much longer Galloping Goose Trail.

Location
Johnson Street bridge, downtown Victoria.

Length
1.5 – 2 hours round trip with possible extension to either Swan Lake Nature Sanctuary (see Walk 24 or further along the Goose.)

Level Easy.

Special attractions
Views of the Inner Harbour and Selkirk waterfront; the 300 metre-long Selkirk trestle; a short side trail along Cecelia Creek.

How to get there
Follow Johnson Street to its bridge over the Inner Harbour. Walk across the bridge by the Via Rail station platform.

THE WALK Having walked to the end of the **station platform** continue another 50 metres and turn right down a two way paved trail. This is the beginning of the CRD's Galloping Goose Regional Trail. The trail initially passes a number of buildings including the **Point Hope shipyard** on the right before entering a more open stretch with views of the Inner Harbour on one side and some **Victoria West** hillside homes on the other.

At two kilometres the trail veers right to pass over the 300 metre long **Selkirk trestle**. Before the trestle however, on the left is a historical interpretive sign and also an access trail to the small waterside **Banfield Park**. Once over the trestle a walkway to the right leads to the **Selkirk waterfront** — a mixture of office and residential buildings including a café or two.

The Goose continues straight and soon passes under the Gorge Road Bridge. **Cecelia Creek**, which once supported fish, wildlife and plants drains into the Inner Harbour at this point. Although only a few

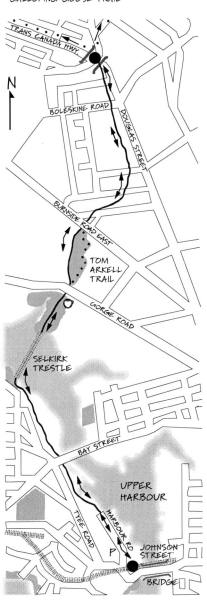

GALLOPING GOOSE TRAIL

13

hundred metres of the creek remain exposed, the city of Victoria is attempting to revitalize it and has constructed the **Tom Arkell Trail** along its banks. This trail runs parallel to the Goose before crossing the creek by a flat wooden bridge. The trail joins the Goose a hundred metres further on as it re-crosses the creek over a wide concrete and stone bridge.

After the Goose passes under **Burnside Road** there follows a series of intersections as it winds through an industrial section of the city. The **Switch Bridge** over the **Trans-Canada Highway** is reached just before the four kilometre sign. The bridge, the km marker and an interpretive sign marks the turning of the Goose west toward Sooke and its terminus at Leechtown, and the beginning of the Lochside Trail going north to Sidney.

The walk ends here but walkers can continue on either trail for a longer outing. (The Goose parallels the Trans-Canada Highway for the next six kilometres. It's rather noisy and not the most scenic portion of the trail. **Lochside Trail**, within half a kilometre of the Switch Bridge, passes by and offers access to the **Swan Lake Nature Sanctuary**. See Walk 24.) •

Selkirk trestle as the Goose crosses over Selkirk Water

5 THE GORGE WATERWAY

The present day Gorge Water-way is roughly a two-kilometre tidal passage that connects Selkirk Water with Portage Inlet — a much longer stretch of water which has its beginning at Victoria's Inner Harbour. For well over a hundred years this pictur-esque waterway has been a favourite recreational area for Victorians. The Kinsmen Gorge Park on its southern bank had its beginnings as the BC Electric Railway Gorge Amusement Park which, at its opening in July of 1905, attracted an estimated 4000 people most of whom arrived in the #5 streetcar from Victoria.

On the right of the entrance to the park are fifteen Japanese flowering cherry trees. They were planted in 1995 to com-memorate both the destruction of the park's Japanese garden and the removal of all Japanese people from the West Coast during World War II.

General description
A mostly flat scenic walk that takes in the Gorge Waterway, a small park and two historic sites.

Location
Four kilometres north-west of downtown Victoria straddling the municipalities of Saanich and Esquimalt.

Length 1 hour loop.

Level Easy

Special attractions
The picturesque Gorge Waterway; picnic tables in Kinsmen Park; Japanese flowering cherry trees; the historic Craigflower Schoolhouse and Kosapsom Park.

How to get there
From downtown take Douglas Street for almost two kilometres to its junction with Gorge Road. Turn left onto Gorge Road and after two kilo-metres, turn left at the traffic light at Tillicum Road. Immediately the road passes over the Gorge Bridge. Turn right after the bridge into the drive-way to Kinsmen Gorge Park. Pass through the gate driving the short distance to the carpark. *(Bus #10 Gorge and #26 Crosstown.)*

THE WALK Take the path at the carpark's north side to the water's edge turning left to follow the white chain fence. Continue for 100 metres through a children's play area and then over a wooden bridge to **Sioux Place** — a residential cul-de-sac. Walk the 70 metres up Sioux to **Craigflower Road** and turn right. Walk along the road's sidewalk as it winds and undulates to the junction of **Admirals Road**. Turn right on Admirals and, after 30 metres, cross the **metal railed bridge** that separates the Gorge from Portage Inlet.

Pass the historic Craigflower schoolhouse (built in 1855) and immediately descend to the right into Kosapsom Park — a small grassy picnic and play area which was the home of the Kosapsom First Nations people well before any white settlers. (Archeological remains found in the area date back 2,400 years).

Walk through the park heading for the wide pathway of the **Gorge Waterway** 70 metres away. Turn right onto the waterway path following it along its trim white chained fence for over a kilometre before it

GORGE WATERWAY

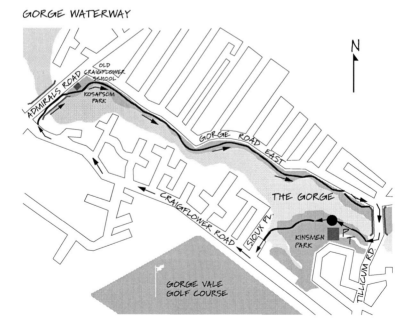

descends to the water on a gravel path. After 100 metres it emerges at the junction of **Tillicum** and **Gorge Roads.** Turn right and walk over the Gorge Bridge taking the narrow paved path beside the bridge back into the **Kinsmen Gorge Park**. Keep to this path as it descends to the water. Turn left at the water following the familiar white chain fence back to the carpark. •

. . . .

6 JAMES BAY

This walk will take you into the heart of tourist land. However, I think it's worth it especially if it's done on one of those lazy Sunday afternoons in spring before the crowds come.

In the mid to late 1800s James Bay was transformed from a large, bucolic farm into Victoria's most fashionable suburb. Businessmen and local politicians bought sizeable tracts of land to build grand homes with long driveways and formal gardens. Over time these landowners moved east to the Rockland area and their properties became sub-divided. The character of the neighbourhood changed as

smaller houses and a profusion of streets were built. Today, James Bay has a charm of its own with some fine examples of cozy "widows' cottages" and restored original larger houses.

General description
An urban walk around the scenic and historic neighbourhood of James Bay.

Location
West and south of downtown

Length 1 hour

Level Easy

Special attractions
Close to downtown; ocean and mountain views; Fisherman's Wharf; breakwater excursion; Ogden Point Café; historic Government Street.

THE WALK Walk west in front of the **Legislature Buildings** along **Belleville Street** keeping to the water side. Pass the Royal London Wax Museum, the Coho ferry terminal and the Victoria Clipper facility. Immediately after the entrance to the **Clipper parking lot** take a path down to the right. This path goes to the water's edge then follows the shoreline to pass in front of the Laurel Point Hotel through **Laurel Point Park**. The path ends at the far side of the Coast Victoria Harbourside Hotel. Take the lane at the side of the hotel and turn right onto **Kingston Street**. Follow Kingston a short distance until it becomes **St. Lawrence Street**. The entrance to **Fisherman's Wharf** is at this point. The wharf is an interesting collection of people and boats and is home to fishermen, house boaters and sailors. One of Victoria' favourite fish and chips shop is located on the main dock. At the corner of an open playing field turn right on Erie, walk for a block, then turn left on **Dallas Road**.

The walk now passes by the Canadian Coast Guard docks and

Ogden Point Café at the head of the breakwater

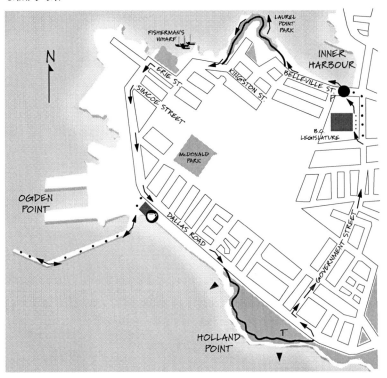

veers south and then east to **Ogden Point** where the Juan de Fuca
Strait and the Olympic Mountains come into view. On a clear day,
Mt. Olympus' snowy peak can be seen through the cleft in the closer
mountains. Ogden Point is Victoria's port facility where merchant and
cruise ships dock. You'll find a good interpretive display near the
terminal building. It also serves as the helicopter terminal of Helijet
Airways. At the head of the point's kilometre-long breakwater is
the **Ogden Point Café** — offering a great opportunity to rest and
replenish, (especially if the walk out and back along the breakwater
has been included).

From the Point continue along the shoreline taking the cliff
path onto the grassy **Holland Point**. When the path rejoins **Dallas
Road** cross to the north side of the road and retreat for a block to
Government Street. Turn right here.

Government Street is one of Victoria's landmarks being flanked by the Empress Hotel, the Royal B.C. Museum and the B.C. Legislature. Here, at its southern reaches, are fine examples of Victorian residential architecture. **Number 140** Government is the residence known as "Woodlands" thought to date from 1861. At the right-hand corner of Government and Simcoe Streets is **Carr House**, birthplace of Victoria's well known artist and writer Emily Carr. (Carr's residence for many years, "House of All Sorts" still exists at 40 Simcoe Street, east of Government).

On the left side and closer to the Legislature at Michigan Street is a handsomely-restored Victorian home — now a bed and breakfast — the **Holland House Inn**. At the junction with Superior Street are the rear buildings and garden of the Legislature. You can finish the walk either on Government Street or by passing through the right portal at the side of the Legislature Building down to the Inner Harbour. •

. . . .

7 MOSS ROCK PARK

Including Beacon Hill Park, the seawall & Fairfield district

Beacon Hill Park is almost as old as Victoria itself. The Hudson's Bay Company had established Fort Victoria in 1843 and by 1846 had named the present parcel of land Beacon Hill because of the two beacons erected on the hill for navigational purposes. It was not until 1882 however, that the provincial government gave the park in trust to the city of Victoria.

On the eastern border of the park is the district of Fairfield. Until the land-boom before the First World War, Fairfield was comprised of small farms and market gardens. Like other areas

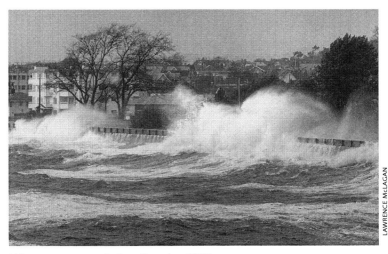

Winter storm waves in Ross Bay, circa 1987

of the city such as James Bay and Rocklands, initially the larger parcels of land were divided into ten-acre estates where some of the city's famous had their residences including Joseph Trutch, Matthew Begbie, Thomas Shotbolt and Augustus Pemberton. Then in the early 1900s, subdivisions reduced the area into lines of small lots along a network of intersecting streets. Still, today the area has much to offer the resident and visitor. Its easy access to parks and ocean, its well-maintained homes and gardens and the unexpected landmark of Moss Rock make Fairfield a special part of the city.

General description

A walk in a mixture of parkland, quiet, attractive house-and-garden-lined streets, a rocky outcrop and oceanfront.

Location

Beacon Hill Park and the district of Fairfield.

Length 2 hours

Level

Easy with some scrambling at Moss Rock Park if desired.

Special attractions

Beautiful Beacon Hill Park; quiet streets; spectacular views in all directions from Moss Rock; Moss Rock Café at Moss and May; seawall and cliff-side walk; Beacon Hill Park's Children's Farm.

21

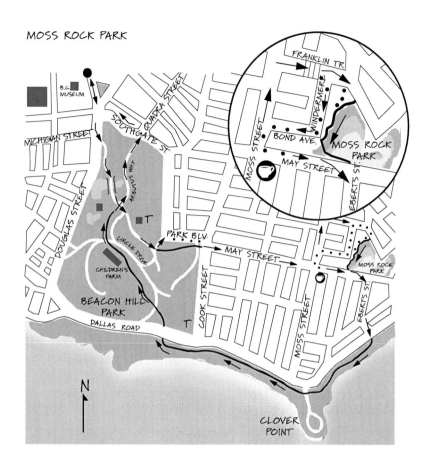

THE WALK This walk has its start at the rear of the **Empress Hotel** on **Douglas Street**. Turn right on Douglas and walk south crossing Belleville Street keeping **Thunderbird Park** and **Helmcken House** on the right. **Beacon Hill Park** has its northern extremity at the corner of Douglas and Superior Streets, one block up the hill from Belleville. Cross Superior and walk for one block crossing Douglas at **Michigan Street** and entering the park on **Bridge Way** directly opposite Michigan.

This access to the park is closed to vehicular traffic so don't be alarmed by the metal barriers at the entrance. Bridge Way derives its name from the stone bridge erected in 1889 to cross **Goodacre Lake** and traverses the park in an east-west direction.

After passing **Arbutus Way** on the left and the park washrooms, also on the left, the road intersects **Heywood Way** directly opposite the cricket pitch. Turn left here, cross the road and, after 20 to 30 metres turn right either on **Park Boulevard** or on the path that runs parallel to Park Boulevard but is separated by a line of trees and bushes. This path passes close to the park's **bowling greens** and ends, as does Park Boulevard, at **Cook Street**.

Cross Cook by the nearby pedestrian crossing at **May Street** and walk east along May for five blocks turning left at **Moss Street** (**Moss Street Café** is situated at this intersection). Cross Moss and take the third street on the right which is **Franklin Terrace**. Although marked as a no-exit street there is a pathway and short flight of stairs at its top right corner which leads to **Windermere Place**. Cross Windermere and walk straight ahead for 30 metres turning right at the **Moss Rock Park** sign on **Masters Road**. Moss Rock Park is 50 metres along Masters on the right.

The mass of Moss Rock itself is an easy scramble of five or so vertical metres and offers unimpeded views of the city and far beyond. For those not up to the scramble, there are **two benches** placed at the base of the rock with south-facing vistas.

The return route begins just below the lowest of these two benches and is the way down to May Street. This is not a path rather a route of approximately 30 metres that can easily be followed by virtue of the worn rock and grass. This climb down is a little tricky especially when wet but is very manageable. The bottom of the climb ends abruptly on May Street opposite **Eberts Street** and the Stewart Memorial Works building. (See end of walk description for alternate return routes). Cross May and walk down Eberts to the ocean at **Dallas Road**.

Walk across Dallas to the water side and, instead of turning right up the hill, take the opening slightly to the left which marks the beginning of the lower **seawall walkway** to **Clover Point**. After 300 metres at the entrance to Clover Point cross the entrance road and walk to the cliff path beyond. Continue west along this path until 50 metres past the intersection of **Dallas** and **Cook Streets** turning right along the path in front of a stand of cottonwood trees.

Cross Dallas at this point by the pedestrian crossing and walk up the asphalt path to the **totem pole** directly ahead. Once the world's tallest, the pole was erected in memory of those First Nations men who fought and died in the two world wars. Walk left past the pole to join, and then turn right on, **Circle Drive**. You'll find it safest to cross to the south side of the road walking on a discernible path to the **Children's Farm** two hundred metres on the left. Re-cross Circle Drive at the farm turning left in front of the putting green and the **Robbie Burns Memorial** statue.

Turn right after 30 metres along the **Park Way** footpath. Pass by the Cameron Memorial Pavilion (an open-air concert pavilion extensively used during the summer months) on the left and at the path's end cross over Bridge Way taking Arbutus Way down past Goodacre Lake to the park entrance at the junction of **Quadra** and **Southgate Streets**. Turn left and cross Southgate walking a block to Douglas Street. Turn right on Douglas walking down the hill back to the Empress.

For those not wanting to take the above-described return route to the Empress here are two suggestions for **alternative routes**.

One is to simply retrace the outward route to Moss Rock as outlined.

The second is to join the described return route via an easier way (avoiding the climbing route down to May Street). Walk back to **Masters Road** turning left on Windermere. Follow Windermere as it winds down to the right to join **Bond Street**. Turn right on Bond and left on Moss Street. In one block Moss intersects May Street. Turn left on May and cross the road walking three blocks to **Eberts Street**. Turn right on Eberts and join the previously-described return route via the water front and Beacon Hill Park. •

8 THREE PEAKS

(Anderson Hill Park, Walbran Park & Gonzales Hill Regional Park)

I call this the Three Peaks walk because it takes us up and over three attractive hills tucked away in the south-eastern corner of Oak Bay. Situated between Gonzales and McNeill Bays this spectacular piece of land origi-nally belonged to the Ross family back in the 1840s. It was later subdivided into small lots where wealthy Victorians built their summer cottages. Today, although crammed with tasteful family homes — most with superb ocean views — the area includes three small pockets of land preserved for us all as parks: Gonzales Hill Regional Park, Wal-bran Park and Anderson Hill Park.

Gonzales Hill, at over 70 metres above sea level, was chosen by the federal govern-ment in 1914 as an ideal site for a weather station and observatory. Originally manned it is now fully automated and comprises part of the small regional district park which bears its name.

Walbran Park was named after Captain John Walbran, the author of British Columbia Coast Names. *The cairn, or as the locals refer to it, "the pike", at the top of Walbran was erected as a monument to the British, Spanish and American explorers of the Strait of Juan de Fuca.*

Locally referred to as Blueberry Hill, Anderson Hill Park was named for the nine-teenth century explorer, agricul-turist, artist and Victoria's first

Walbran cairn above McNeill Bay

JOHN CROUCH

postmaster, Alexander Caulfield Anderson. The Oak Bay municipality purchased the 2.55-hectare piece of land in 1974 and created the park in 1979.

All three of these "peaks" are striking examples of what Victoria has to offer its residents and visitors in the form of high rocky outcrops with outstanding views of city, coast, islands and mountains.

General description

A hilly walk encompassing three high-level city peaks with magnificent views. Not for those who dislike steps — 120 of them.

Location

On the border of the municipalities of Victoria and Oak Bay at the southern tip of the Victoria peninsula.

Length 1.5 to 2 hours.

Level Moderate to strenuous.

Special attraction

Gonzales weather station known as the "Observatory"; views south and west; wonderful spot to see the sunset; Walbran cairn — a monument to exploration with 360 degree views; Anderson Hill Park — a small park with big views.

How to get there

Leave town on Fort Street turning right on Cook Street. Follow Cook to Fairfield and turn left. Take Fairfield for about two kilometres where it becomes Beach Drive. Continue on Beach and 500 metres after it turns left to follow McNeill Bay, park on the ocean side between St. Patrick Street and Transit Road. *(Bus #1 Richardson.)*

THE WALK Begin with **Anderson Hill Park**. From the intersection of **Transit Road** and **Beach Drive** walk up Transit on its right-hand side for 40 metres taking a trail with stairs on the right. After a few metres the trail forks. Take the right fork and follow this rough trail as it twists through bushes and trees until it enters the park through a grove of stunted and windswept Garry oaks. The trail then opens onto a large grass and rock area.

Here, at the summit of the park are **benches, gorse bushes** and **grand views of ocean and mountains. Trial Island** sits just below to the right in the deepening water of **McNeill Bay** (earlier known as Shoal Bay). Return from the summit along a chip trail to the wooden entrance gateway to the park. Turn left on the roadway (**Island Road**)

THREE PEAKS

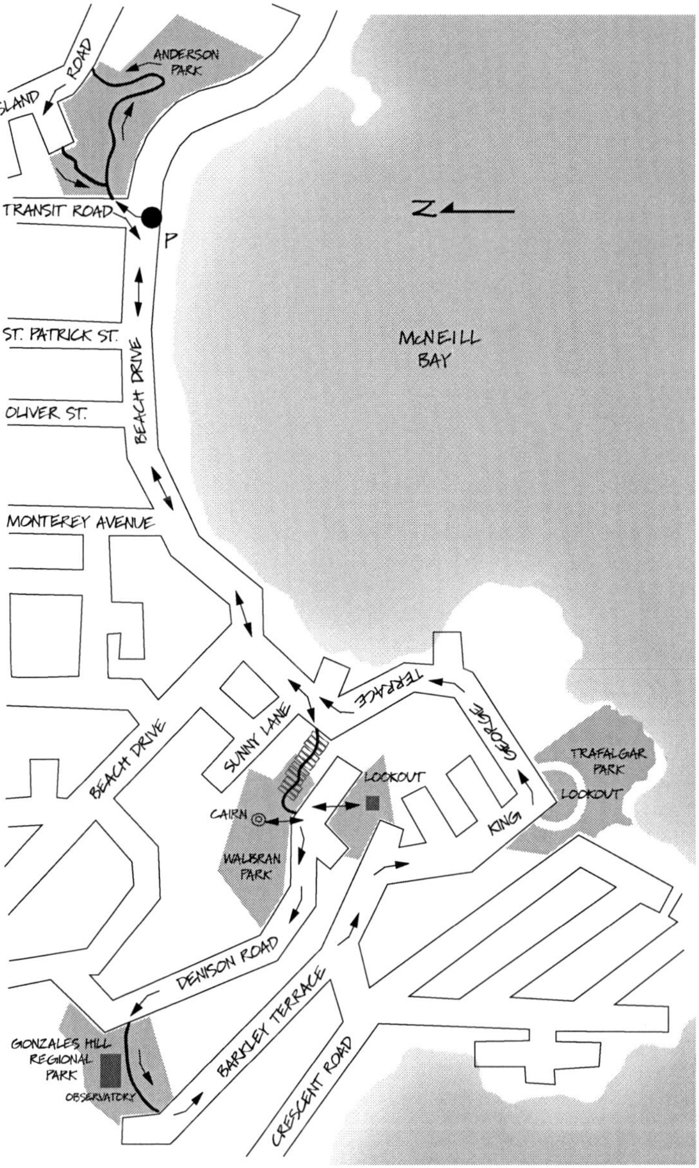

ISLAND ROAD

ANDERSON PARK

TRANSIT ROAD

P

ST. PATRICK ST.

OLIVER ST.

BEACH DRIVE

MONTEREY AVENUE

McNEILL BAY

N

BEACH DRIVE

SUNNY LANE

TERRACE

GEORGE

CAIRN

LOOKOUT

WALBRAN PARK

KING

TRAFALGAR PARK

LOOKOUT

DENISON ROAD

BARKLEY TERRACE

GONZALES HILL REGIONAL PARK

OBSERVATORY

CRESCENT ROAD

and after 100 metres turn left on a lane between two houses (opposite house numbers **597** and **627**). The lane soon becomes a trail and at a trail junction turn right down to **Transit Road**. Turn left here and walk back to **Beach Drive**.

At Beach turn right and walk west toward the junction of **King George Terrace** and Beach. Bear left up King George Terrace. **Sunny Lane** is 40-odd metres to the right. At the corner of Sunny Lane and the Terrace take the flight of stairs marked **"Pathway to Walbran Park"**. This stairway rises almost 70 metres via the steps to the cairn and bunker of Walbran Park.

As you reach the top of the stairs you'll see the bunker across the road (**Dennison Road**). The cairn is on the right about 20 metres past the stairs. Both these landmarks give unimpeded spectacular, 360 degree views of the city, ocean and mountains.

From the cairn turn right on **Dennison Road** and walk 200 metres to the carpark of **Gonzales Hill Regional Park**. Walk left into the carpark and, at its left corner, follow the path to the white building of the **observatory**. Walk left around the building and, after taking in the magnificent views from this over 70 metre above sea level hill, descend the rocky path to **Barkley Terrace**. Turn left on Barkley, walking down the steep hill to **King George Terrace**.

At King George turn left, cross the road and climb to the Terrace's lookout. Directly below is **Harling Point** and the **Chinese Cemetery**. To the left is **Trial Island** (again) and the crescent of McNeill Bay. Leave the lookout and continue along the descending curve of the terrace to its junction with **Beach Drive**. Turn right on Beach and walk the short distance back to the parking area. ●

Garry oak and rock outcropping

9 UVIC, MOUNT TOLMIE & HENDERSON PARK (2 walks)

Once the site of an army camp, the University of Victoria has become, over the past 40 years, a beautifully-designed and landscaped campus. But it could have been otherwise. Back in 1959 when Victoria College needed to expand its campus on Lansdowne Road (now Camosun College) the college's development board decided to ask a San Francisco architectural and planning company for some advice.

The company suggested that rather than expand the Lansdowne campus it should move lock, stock and barrel to the newly acquired Gordon Head military camp. Despite some stiff resistance the suggestion was eventually accepted by the college's council and the process of creating the University of Victoria began. Today, what we see is a central ring road with almost all the academic buildings situated within its circumference. Outside are the student union buildings, the faculty club, student residences, the gymnasium, the Centennial Stadium, plus many hectares of undeveloped woods and grassland. And for the walker there is the Alumni Trail — a gravel and chip trail that circles the campus, and the delight of Mystic Vale.

To the southwest of the university is Mount Tolmie Park — a 120 metre-high hill named after William Frazer Tolmie, a prominent nineteenth century Victoria physician and legislator.

Henderson Park is home to both a recreation centre and a nine-hole, par-three golf course. This 8.5-hectare park has a kilometre-long chip trail that winds through the woods surrounding the golfing greens.

General description
A choice of two loop walks offering a contrast of landscapes including rock outcrops, a deep ravine, formal gardens, woods and university campus buildings.

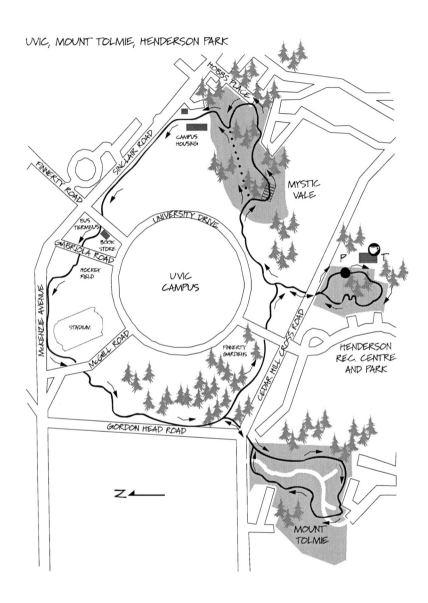

Location

Seven kilometres north-east of Victoria's centre on the borders of Saanich and Oak Bay municipalities.

Length

Complete loop: 2 hours
University loop only: 1.5 hours

Level Easy to moderate.

Special attractions

Mystic Vale — an ecological preserve ravine within the UVic campus; 360-degree views of the city, mountains and ocean from the summit of Mount Tolmie; Henderson Park's mini-golf course and coffee shop.

How to get there

From downtown travel on Blanshard Street for two kilometres turning right on Hillside Avenue. At the fifth set of traffic lights (Shelbourne Street) Hillside becomes Lansdowne Road. Turn left at the second set of traffic lights past Shelbourne onto Henderson Road. After a kilometre turn right at the traffic light onto Cedar Hill Cross Road. The entrance to Henderson Park and Recreation Centre and parking lot is just past the tennis courts 300 metres on the right. (Bus #4 UVic.)

THE WALK From the **Henderson** parking lot walk on the **golf course** side of the park to the recreation centre entrance. Continue past the entrance to take the good chip trail circling the golf course in a clockwise direction. The trail borders the park for almost 400 metres then begins to weave among the greens before paralleling **Cedar Hill Cross Road**. Just as the trail turns right to parallel the road, take the short exit trail to the left onto the road's sidewalk.

Cross the road diagonally to the left and enter the university's **Alumni Trail** through the trees by a power pole. After a hundred metres or so the trail forks and then forks again a few metres further. Follow the right-turning trail in both instances. The trail soon brushes the **university's ring road** as it curves to the right. Ignore a trail on the left following the trail as it turns right to border a large parking lot. At the first corner of the parking lot turn right at a trail junction walking 30 metres to a trail going left. This trail soon descends into a ravine by a long flight of steps.

This is **Mystic Vale**. (To bypass Mystic Vale see * below.) Turn left at the bottom following the creek bed as it flows eastward toward

Sinclair Road and Cadboro Bay. After about 600 metres the tail rises quickly and ends at the paved cul-de-sac of Hobbs Place. Look for another trail five metres off to the left. Walk up this steady incline to join a narrow paved road that passes a cluster of single-storey university buildings. Again, look for a paved and chipped trail going to the right. Cross a small parking lot of another building and then cross in front of recently erected university accommodation (on your left) to emerge onto Sinclair Road.**

Turn left on the paved sidewalk of Sinclair and climb the hill to Finnerty Road. Turn left on Finnerty crossing it to walk between the bus terminus and the campus bookstore. Follow the sidewalk to the right of McKinnon Gymnasium and cross Gabriola Road to the trail that runs beside the all-weather hockey field. Continue following the trail as it turns left down the slight hill of McKenzie Avenue. The trail then curves left at the north end of Centennial Stadium to cross McGill Road — a main entry to the campus — and over a grassy area into the woods beyond.

Tracing a winding course, the trail crosses a flat wooden bridge and then gradually rises through a wooded area to a large parking lot situated on the left. Cross the entrance road walking 50 metres up the gravel trail to a junction. This is the beginning of the route to Mount Tolmie. (To by-pass the Mount Tolmie portion of this walk and to complete the University loop only, continue straight at this point following the trail as it winds toward University Drive. See *** below for trail description.) Turn right at the junction along the lighted path that leads to the corner of Cedar Hill Cross Road and Gordon Head Road. Cross Cedar Hill Cross Road at the light-controlled pedestrian crossing to the Mount Tolmie trail directly opposite.

TO MOUNT TOLMIE At the trail marker climb steeply keeping to the left-hand trail along the south-east side of the park. Ignore the trail intersecting from the right at about 50 metres. The trail bears left and climbs even more steeply as it passes a large rock outcropping on the

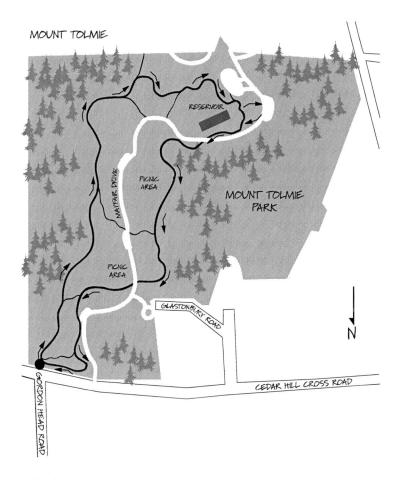

MOUNT TOLMIE

RESERVOIR

MAYFAIR DRIVE

PICNIC AREA

MOUNT TOLMIE PARK

PICNIC AREA

GLASTONBURY ROAD

N

GORDON HEAD ROAD

CEDAR HILL CROSS ROAD

left. The Garry oaks at this point are sparse and stunted but a short distance beyond the trail winds through a thicker grove. The trail emerges from this grove and continues upward taking a left fork and then a right fork as it twists towards the summit. Soon the **summit reservoir** comes into view with the trail going to its left. Climb a short flight of steps and then bear right to the summit proper. Across the road is the **Mount Tolmie Lookout** with views to the south of the city, the **Sooke Hills** and the **Olympic Mountains**.

Walk off the rocks by a rough path and take the gravel path in front of the reservoir that leads to the road going down to the right. Cross the road following it for 50 metres before taking the trail down between two picnic tables. The trail descends steeply winding on the western edge of the park. **Mount Douglas** is visible straight ahead. At a picnic area the trail forks right. Keep the road to the right until, just before **Glastonbury Road**, the trail turns right and crosses the paved road. Shortly after the crossing bear left at a fork and descend the trail paralleling the road down to **Cedar Hill Cross Road**. At Cedar Hill turn right and walk the 40 metres to the light-controlled pedestrian crossing.

Re-cross Cedar Hill Cross Road and return along the lighted trail to the trail junction. Turn right on the good trail that curves its way to **University Drive**.*** With a wide grassy area bordering Cedar Hill Cross Road the trail passes a signed trail on the left that heads into the university's **Finnerty Gardens**. (There are myriad paths in the gardens and is a worthwhile side tour for those interested). Thirty metres or so after the garden's entrance the trail meets and crosses University Drive to continue through a thickly-wooded area.

After another 100 metres there are two trail junctions 20 metres apart. Take the right trail in both instances. Another 100 metres or so the trail crosses **Cedar Hill Cross Road** and enters the **Henderson Park** trail at the same point as at the walk's beginning. Turn left and walk the short distance back to the car park.

JAMES R. SMITH

Magnolia

*To bypass **Mystic Vale** turn left at this point taking the path through the woods parallel to the parking lot. The trail crosses a paved lane and onto a small parking area to the right of a single-storey building and then passes in front of recently-erected university accommodation (on your left) to join Sinclair Road. Follow the description for the rest of the walk from Sinclair Road, marked ** above. •

10 WEST BAY MARINA TO CAIRN PARK

Esquimalt's early history is dominated by two quite divergent activities: one naval, the other agricultural. Because of its excellent harbour, Esquimalt was chosen, in 1865, by the British Navy as the permanent naval base for its Pacific fleet. Fifteen years before this naval occupation the Hudson's Bay Company's subsidiary, the Puget Sound Agricultural Company, had established Viewfield Farm, the first of four farms in the Esquimalt area. (The others being Constance Cove, Craigflower and Colwood Farms.)

The legacy of these two developments has had a profound effect on the township of Esquimalt. It is now known the world over as Canada's Pacific naval base and the early farms have been used to create some of the area's most picturesque and distinctive neighbourhoods.

The five parks that you'll walk through were once part of Viewfield Farm. The first,

Macauley Point Park, is named after the farm's first manager, Donald Macauley. He died by drowning in Esquimalt's harbour in 1868. Saxe Point Park derives its name from Queen Victoria's consort, Prince Albert. His family name was Saxe-Colburg. The small Buxton Green Park at the side of the Fleming Beach boat ramp was once the site of Victoria's first natural saltwater swimming pool. Named to recognize early settlers of Esquimalt, the Buxton family, the park was opened in 1983. Highrock or Cairn Park is the municipality's highest point at a little over 70 metres (232.25 ft.). The paved path to and from the cairn itself follows the survey line that once divided the old Viewfield and Constance Cove farms.

General description

A loop walk that takes in three waterfront parks; downtown Esquimalt and the municipality's highest spot — Cairn Park.

Location

Ten minutes by car from downtown Victoria in the municipality of Esquimalt.

Length 2 hours

Level Easy to moderate

Special attractions

Macauley Point Park, site of the late 19th century earthwork Battery and Fort; Saxe Point Park; (Both give views of ocean, mountains, Metchosin and the Sooke peninsula.) tide pools; Memorial and Cairn Parks. (The latter having a history that dates back to the late eighteen hundreds.)

THE WALK Before taking the short **Gore Street** to turn left on **Lyall Street** notice the Italianate-styled house next to **West Bay Park**. Built in 1893 for Captain Victor Jacobson and his wife its style has also been called **Steamboat Gothic**. *(See photo)* Cross Lyall and immediately turn right onto **Peters Street**. (You

How to get there

Take Johnson Street going west over the "blue bridge" to Esquimalt Road. Follow Esquimalt Road for two kilometres turning left onto Head Street. After two blocks park either in the West Bay Walk parking area on the left or just past Gore Street opposite the tiny West Bay Park. In the summer, it is possible to take the Inner Harbour ferry from the marina below the Empress Hotel to West Bay Marina and to begin the walk there. *(Bus #25 Munro.)*

JOHN CROUCH

are now on Department of National Defense property. As it is mostly housing you are free to walk within its boundaries.)

A line of four horse-chestnut trees mark the beginning of Peters, a street which ends at the junction with **Bewdley Avenue**. Turn right on Bewdley and after a hundred metres turn left on **Anson Street**. Walk downhill to the end of Anson and, as it crosses **Vaughan Street** to become **Anson Crescent**, take the gravel path on the right a few metres on Anson Crescent down toward the ocean.

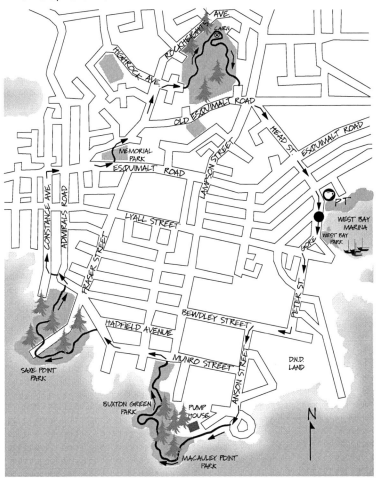

Pass in front of the **pumping station** and walk on the paved path into **Macauley Point Park**. (Site of the 19th century Battery and Fort Macauley.) This path keeps close to the water and is liberally supplied with viewing benches. Throughout this headland park there are wonderful views of the Strait of Juan de Fuca, the Olympic Mountains, the Metchosin shoreline and the Sooke peninsula. Along this winding path there are a number of beach access trails and spots for picnicking. **Tide pools** are plentiful when the tide is right.

As the path nears **Fleming Park** several rough tracks to the right lead up to viewing bunkers at the top of the point. (The actual path that leads to the bunkers is on the northeast side of the park.) Stay on this main path and, as it becomes a concrete surface, turn right walking past the small **Buxton Green Park** and onto the roadway of the **Fleming Beach boat ramp**.

Exit the boat ramp and turn left onto **Munro Street**. Two hundred metres along Munro take the trail on the right almost opposite **Hadfield Street**. This trail leads into **Saxe Point Park**. Keep to the left trail which soon opens onto some low bluffs with a scattering of defiant wind-ravaged firs. This trail peters out as it meets the well-maintained grass of the park. Walk toward the **flagpole** and then across the parking lot to take a narrow gravel and chip trail that goes to the left into a wooded area. With the water on your left continue along this path, avoiding side trails, as it gently rises toward **Bewdley Avenue**.

LAWRENCE McLAGAN

Saxe Point

At Bewdley turn left walking the few metres to **Admirals Road**. At the corner of Bewdley and Admirals take the narrow paved path on the left that takes you down to **Constance Avenue**. The charm of Esquimalt is exemplified on this street as cottage-style homes snuggle together behind small, neat gardens. Turn right on Constance walking the two blocks to **Esquimalt Road**. Turning right on Esquimalt walk to the crosswalk on the **Tudor House Inn** side of Admirals Road.

Cross Esquimalt Road by the crosswalk and turn right. A short distance away is the entrance to **Memorial Park**. Walk through the park passing the cenotaph built to commemorate the residents of Esquimalt who fought and died in the First World War. Exit the park on **Park Terrace** and turn right. Cross the street and walk the few metres to **Old Esquimalt Road**. Follow this road as it ascends to the left before turning left onto **Rockheights Avenue**. (Notice the art deco-style houses on the right going up the hill.) Once on Rockheights watch for and turn right on **Highrock Avenue** and the sign pointing to **Cairn Park**.

At the junction of **Highrock Avenue** and **Highrock Place** follow the signed footpath going to the left and climb the flight of steps into Cairn Park. Almost 50 metres past the steps take the rough trail between the bushes on the left. (You've gone too far if you come to a trail junction and the end of the paved portion of the path.) This trail climbs unevenly over a rocky route (not steep) for less than 100 metres joining a paved path up to the cairn, **Esquimalt's highest point**. From the cairn retrace the paved path following it down through a field to the very short, no-exit, **Cairn Place**.

The plaque at the corner of Cairn Place and Old Esquimalt Road (park side) explains why the park was previously known as **"The Transfer"**. Cross Old Esquimalt Road and walk left to cross **Lampson Street**. Over Lampson take the well-signed **Head Street**. Continue down Head crossing **Esquimalt Road, Wollaston** and **Dunsmuir Streets** back to the walk's start. •

11 WEST BAY

The inscription at the base of the totem pole on the northern shore of Victoria's Inner Harbour is titled Westsong Way — *a nice poetic reference to the Songhees First Nation who had occupied the site until the early 1900s. The Songhees band had moved from its Cadboro Bay location in the mid 1800s to settle in the Inner Harbour. But in 1911 the provincial government of the day bought the land from the Songhees ostensibly to provide Victoria with a railway terminal and a harbour facility. Only the terminal materialized. Still known today as the "Songhees", the land is primarily a residential area and, thanks to good planning, is the beginning of a two and half kilometre walkway to West Bay Marina in Esquimalt.*

General description

An easy walk along the north side of the Victoria harbour to the West Bay Marina starting from the Empress Hotel.

Location

North of the downtown Inner Harbour.

Length

1 hour 15 minutes — round trip

Level Easy

Special attractions

Views of Inner Harbour, Empress Hotel, Legislature, Laurel and Shoal Points; activities of the busy harbour with its boats and aircraft; refreshments at West Bay Marina and Spinnaker's Pub; option of a ferry ride for the return trip.

JAMES R. SMITH

Time for a "quick one"?

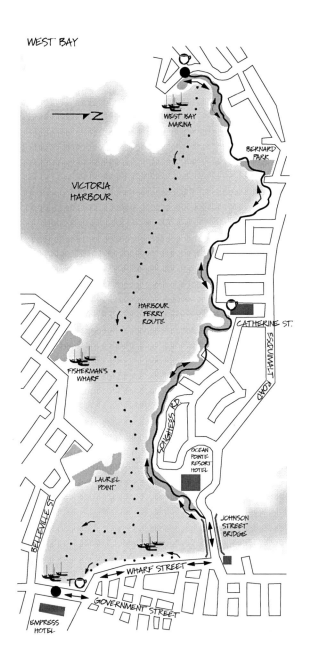

WEST BAY

WEST BAY
MARINA

BERNARD
PARK

VICTORIA
HARBOUR

HARBOUR
FERRY
ROUTE

CATHERINE ST.

FISHERMAN'S
WHARF

SONGHEES RD

TYEE ROAD

OCEAN
POINTE
RESORT
HOTEL

LAUREL
POINT

JOHNSON
STREET
BRIDGE

BELLEVILLE ST.

WHARF STREET

GOVERNMENT STREET

EMPRESS
HOTEL

THE WALK Starting from the **Empress Hotel** walk across to the **Inner Harbour** and turn right (north) taking the first left at the tourism centre along **Wharf Street**. (This walk will always have the water on the left outward bound). Walk along Wharf Street on the water side. The store fronts between **Fort Street** and **Yates Street** are some of the oldest buildings in the city. **Number 1107 Wharf Street** (on the town side of the street) for instance, is the building Emily Carr's father, Richard Carr, built in 1862 for his wholesale mercantile business.

After a kilometre turn left and walk over the **Johnson Street bridge** (the "Blue Bridge"), again keeping to the left. Over the bridge take the pathway down to the water's edge and walk in front of the **Ocean Pointe Resort Hotel**. This pathway marks the beginning of the **Westsong Way** and proceeds in a westerly direction terminating at West Bay.

The walkway was constructed in 1990 by the city of Victoria and the municipality of Esquimalt along with the development of the Songhees condominium and townhouse site. The **totem pole** standing just past the hotel was erected to commemorate the fifteenth Commonwealth Games held in Victoria in 1994. Called the **Spirit of Lekwammen** (Spirit of Nations) the pole was a gift to the people of Canada by the Songhees band.

The path winds close to the water in front of the condominiums before joining a short portion of roadway marking the end of the Songhees part of the walk. At the two kilometre mark the path continues along a wide curve and then passes below **Spinnaker's Pub** (a possible halting point on the way back!) at the foot of **Catherine Street**. A flight of concrete steps on the right marks the beginning of a long boardwalk section.

After this first of a few sections of **boardwalk**, the path narrows and meanders through a delightful rocky promontory overlooking **West Bay Marina**. The boardwalk soon resumes again and follows a rather twisting route along the shoreline. The walkway terminates in a wide expanse of decking with benches overlooking the marina.

To extend the walk to the marina, continue past the decking to the road. Turn left and, after a hundred metres, turn left again on **Head Street**. The entrance to the marina is 30 metres from the corner on the left. Refreshments are available at the marina's **Dockside Café**. In the summer months the Inner Harbour **ferry boat** offers a pleasant alternative journey back to the marina in front of the Empress.

If returning to the Empress by foot an attractive detour (apart from a "quick one" at Spinnaker's Pub) is to walk by the waterfront below Wharf Street. After crossing the Johnson Street bridge turn right on Wharf. At a hundred metres take the flight of stairs beside the **Wharfside Eatery Restaurant** down to the water. Turn left and follow the water's edge to the marina in front of the Empress. •

Seawall on the approach to West Bay Marina

Saanich and View Royal

12 BROADMEAD (2 walks)

With the distant hum of the traffic on the Pat Bay Highway less than five hundred metres away, a walker can be deep in a second growth coniferous forest on a winding, sometimes rocky trail heading up to the reservoir atop Cordova Ridge. This forested trail is the first stage of two circular walks that thread their way

JAMES R. SMITH

Second growth forest on the western slopes of Cordova Ridge

through the Saanich suburb of Broadmead.

Broadmead was the name given to the late nineteenth century Victoria businessman R.P. Rithet's 295-hectare farm known both as Rithet's Ranch and Broadmead Farm. The Rithets had a favourite thoroughbred racehorse called Broadmead and it was the horse's name that was affectionately given to the family farm.

Farm life at Broadmead centred around horses, and in particular, racehorses. At any one time a dozen or more horses were stabled at the farm and were put through their paces on the farm's race track which was located on the site of the present day Royal Oak Burial Park.

The plans for the massive suburban development we now know as Broadmead were first created in 1965. Fortunately for local residents and Victorians in general, the plans included 60 hectares of parkland in the more than 280 hectare development. In the almost 40 years of the area's growth those 60 hectares have been jealously guarded by the residents and carefully tended by the municipality's parks department.

General description
These two circular walks pass through thick second-growth forest, rise to the top of Cordova Ridge and meander on well-maintained trails through the heavily treed suburb of Broadmead.

Location
Roughly eight kilometres north of downtown Victoria in the municipality of Saanich.

Length
Walk I: 1 – 1.5 hours
Walk II: 2 – 2.5 hours

Level Moderate

Special attractions
Dense, mainly coniferous forest; ocean and mountain views from Cordova Ridge; a lily pond and Rithet's Bog both with viewing platforms; miniature suburban parks; coffee shops in the shopping centre.

How to get there
Leave town on Blanshard Street. After it becomes the Pat Bay Highway (#17) take the Royal Oak exit turning right onto Royal Oak Drive. At a hundred metres turn right again at the traffic lights into the Broadmead Shopping Centre parking lot. Park close to Royal Oak Drive. (Bus #6 Quadra to Royal Oak.)

WALK 1   From the **Broadmead Shopping Centre** parking lot walk to Royal Oak Drive crossing at the traffic light to **Falaise Drive**. Turn right at the junction of Falaise Drive and Falaise Crescent on to the crescent and either walk diagonally across **Falaise Park** or around the crescent to the "no-exit" **Deventer Drive**.

Turn left here walking 30 metres to the trailhead on the left. This trail soon forks. Take the narrower left trail which quickly becomes rather rocky and twisting as it follows the eastern edge of the **Royal Oak Burial Park**. Cross an intersecting trail and after about 300 metres, at another fork in the trail, in a cluster of tall cedars, take the left-descending trail. This section can be a little boggy in winter but in the summer there's a profusion of horsetails.

The trail then bears right and, after a short climb, descends into an alder-filled gully. Keep on the gully's right side as the trail undulates to the head of the gully where it crosses to the left and begins to climb. Keep left ignoring two side trails and, as the trail swings right, climb straight to the top of the ridge. The trail opens onto a gravel area in front of the **concrete reservoir**. Walking to its right for about 15 metres take the well-defined chip trail of **Grant Park** descending steeply to the right. This trail crosses four roadways before terminating in front of **McMinn Park** on **Lochside Drive**.

Turn right on Lochside walking on its left side. At a set of mail boxes on the right side of the road (opposite Scottswood Lane) take the trail going through the wooded **Kentwood Park**. Continue past a wooden bridge on the right and follow the left-hand trail at a fork walking past the tennis courts. The trail bears left and exits onto **Kentwood Place** cul-de-sac. Walk along Kentwood crossing Amblewood Drive to **Kentwood Terrace**. Walk up and over the Terrace turning left on **Boulderwood Drive**. Walk down Boulderwood to Royal Oak Drive turning right to return to the Broadmead Shopping Centre parking lot.

WALK 2   Follow the above route description to **Lochside Drive**. Instead of turning right through Kentwood Park continue on Lochside

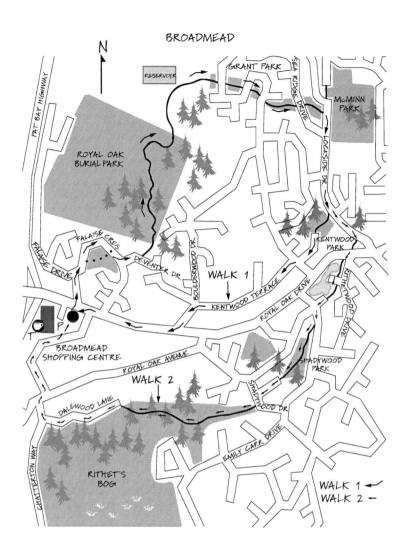

BROADMEAD

to a short trail on the right 30 metres before the intersection with Royal Oak Drive. This trail is interrupted by Royal Oak Drive and continues directly across the road on the right side of **Rithetwood Drive**. The trail now passes a small but well kept pond on the right. This partially shaded pond has water lilies, an island, two small waterfalls and a viewing platform.

Cross **Pondwood Lane** following the trail to **Emily Carr Drive**.

Turn left and at about 50 metres cross the road at the pedestrian crossing and enter **Shadywood Park**. Pass the children's play area and follow the trail through the park and, after 100 metres or so, turn left crossing a stone bridge into the woods. Turn left over the next bridge and turn right on Shadywood Place.

Walk to and cross Shadywood Drive taking the marked trail into **Rithet's Bog**. Continue past the major trail going to the left and skirt the bog in its right side. The trail exits onto **Dalewood Lane**. Walk the lane to **Chatterton Way** (Note viewing platform on Dalewood Lane giving expansive views of the bog.) and turn right. At the top of Chatterton turn left into Broadmead Shopping Centre and its parking lot. ●

· ·

13   CEDAR HILL PARK & GOLF COURSE (2 walks)

Like many a golf course, Cedar Hill was originally a farm. Not surprisingly, given the property's spectacular views, the once thriving dairy farm was named Ocean View Farm by the farm's owners, the McRae family. They kept their 120 milk cows in a barn on the site of the present recreation centre. The original farmhouse is well preserved and used as a volunteer centre. In 1930 the land, then under the ownership of the Hudson's Bay Company, was developed into a 9-hole private golf course. Forty years later the municipality of Saanich bought the land, cleared it extensively and, in 1971 opened both the present 18-hole public golf course with a club house and a recreation centre, indoor tennis facility and playing fields.

General description

A hilly loop trail around the perimeter of an 18-hole golf course. Optional shorter loop.

Location

Three kilometres north-east of downtown Victoria in the municipality of Saanich.

Level Moderate

Length

Main loop: 1 hour
Lower loop: 30 to 45 minutes.

Special attractions

Views of the Juan de Fuca Strait and Olympic Mountains; two large ponds ideal for bird watching; a licensed snack bar in the adjacent recreation centre.

How to get there

From downtown take Fort Street turning left onto Cook Street. Follow Cook for about two kilometres to the lighted junction of Cook and Finlayson Street. Turn right on Finlayson and left at the next street, the light-controlled Cedar Hill Road. The entrance to the recreation centre and trail head is a hundred metres on the left off Cedar Hill Road. *(Bus #24 Cedar Hill.)*

Barwick Lake nestles in the shade on the flanks of Cedar Hill Golf Course

THE WALK From the **recreation centre** parking lot walk to its south-west corner bordering **Finlayson Street** and, crossing the foot-bridge, turn right onto a paved path. This path quickly becomes a grav-el trail and, after 30 metres at a trail junction, turn right to walk the loop trail in a counter-clockwise direction.

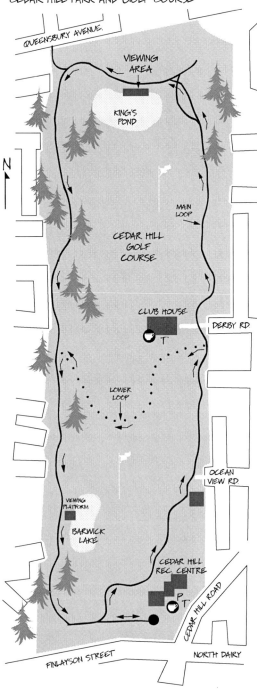

CEDAR HILL PARK AND GOLF COURSE

QUEENSBURY AVENUE.

VIEWING AREA

KING'S POND

N

CEDAR HILL GOLF COURSE

MAIN LOOP

CLUB HOUSE

DERBY RD

LOWER LOOP

OCEAN VIEW RD.

VIEWING PLATFORM

BARWICK LAKE

CEDAR HILL REC. CENTRE

CEDAR HILL ROAD

FINLAYSON STREET

NORTH DAIRY

The trail soon descends and crosses a **wooden bridge** over a seasonal stream. It then follows a wide curve between the indoor tennis courts and the baseball field before ascending very steeply through a sparse grove of tall Garry oak trees. At the top of the rise the trail turns right onto a paved access road which passes directly behind the original **Ocean View Farm farmhouse**. The road bends to the left and, as it exits the park, the gravel path begins again continuing straight ahead up a 200-metre incline.

At the top there is the option of turning left and walking in front of the **club house** to meet the trail on the other side of the golf course for a 1.7k loop or crossing the entrance road to the club house parking lot and continuing up the winding main trail through a bushy and treed area. After 100 metres or so there is a sudden left and then right turn as the trail passes between a line of houses and a row of tall poles with netting used to stop errant golf balls.

The trail then splits into three. Take the middle trail following it as it veers to the left descending to meet a trail coming from the left. Turn right at this junction and continue downhill to pass in front of King's Pond and its viewing area. **King's Pond** is a favourite with local birders as it attracts a variety of wildfowl and other birds throughout the seasons. Around the viewing area there are three inscribed benches donated to the park by different families. The trail rises gently from the pond and takes a southerly direction as it begins its return to the recreation centre. It curves right and then left up a long, winding tree-lined rise.

After a series of turns and undulations the trail descends over a rocky area before straightening and coming to the junction of the cross-golf course trail. Continue straight through a bushy area onto a rocky outcropping and then drop steeply to the park's second pond and viewing platform at **Barwick Lake**. Past the pond the trail soon rises and enters a bramble-bush area by the edge of a row of houses. In the open again, the trail turns sharply left to descend parallel with Finlayson back to the parking lot. •

14 COLQUITZ RIVER PARK

More a creek than a river, the Colquitz waterway and the linear park and trail being established along its banks offer the walker a chance to explore parts of Victoria's suburbs that might otherwise remain hidden.

The name Colquitz is thought to derive from the Esquimalt First Nation phrase "Kwolquitz" or "Kol coagl-quish" meaning "a baby crying". This was the sound the creek was thought to make as it meandered toward Portage Inlet. Some believe it comes from a Celtic word meaning "shaded" or "dark water". Once a prolific trout bearing creek, the Colquitz is now prohibited to fishers.

Back in the late sixties and early seventies when the idea for the park was proposed, the Saanich municipality instigated a stream-enhancement program that included re-stocking the creek with cutthroat trout. The trout now flourish thanks to the improved water quality and the regular re-stocking. With its beginning at the most urban of places — the shopping mall — the trail passes under highway,

JAMES R. SMITH

The patient heron

through housing developments, agricultural wetlands, urban parks and remnants of forest.

Part of the trail passes through a wetland area named Panama Flats. Panama Flats, and its neighbouring hill and pond, was given its name by an English engineer named McDonald. After working on the construction of the Panama Canal in 1904 McDonald bought a 1200-hectare parcel of land in the Carey Road/ Interurban Road area. About 30 hectares were wetland and, reminding McDonald of working in Central America's steaming jungle, he named the area Panama Flats.

General description

A five kilometre long, mostly gravel trail that winds through some interesting residential areas of Saanich.

Location

Six kilometres north of downtown Victoria in the municipality of Saanich.

Length 2 hours out-and-back

Level Easy

Special attractions

An often shaded creekside walk; passes Panama Flats, Hill and Pond — all interesting wildlife viewing spots; opportunities to picnic in urban park settings along the creek; includes Hyacinth and Copley Parks.

How to get there

Take Douglas Street and continue out of town where it becomes the Trans-Canada Highway. After passing under the pedestrian/bicycle bridge (Switch Bridge) as Douglas becomes the highway turn left at the first set of lights onto Tillicum Road. Turn right at the next light onto Burnside Road West and then left again into the parking lot of Tillicum Mall. Park at the right side of the lot between two restaurants and beside the Cuthbert Holmes Park trail. *(Bus #21 Interurban.)*

THE WALK From the Tillicum Mall parking lot access the **Cuthbert Holmes Park** trail and, instead of turning left over the **Colquitz River** on a concrete bridge, continue for a few metres and cross the Trans-Canada Highway off-ramp via the two pedestrian crossings. Walk under the highway and the **Galloping Goose Trail** bridge and, after crossing Burnside Road West, continue on the good gravel trail along the creek.

COLQUITZ RIVER TRAIL

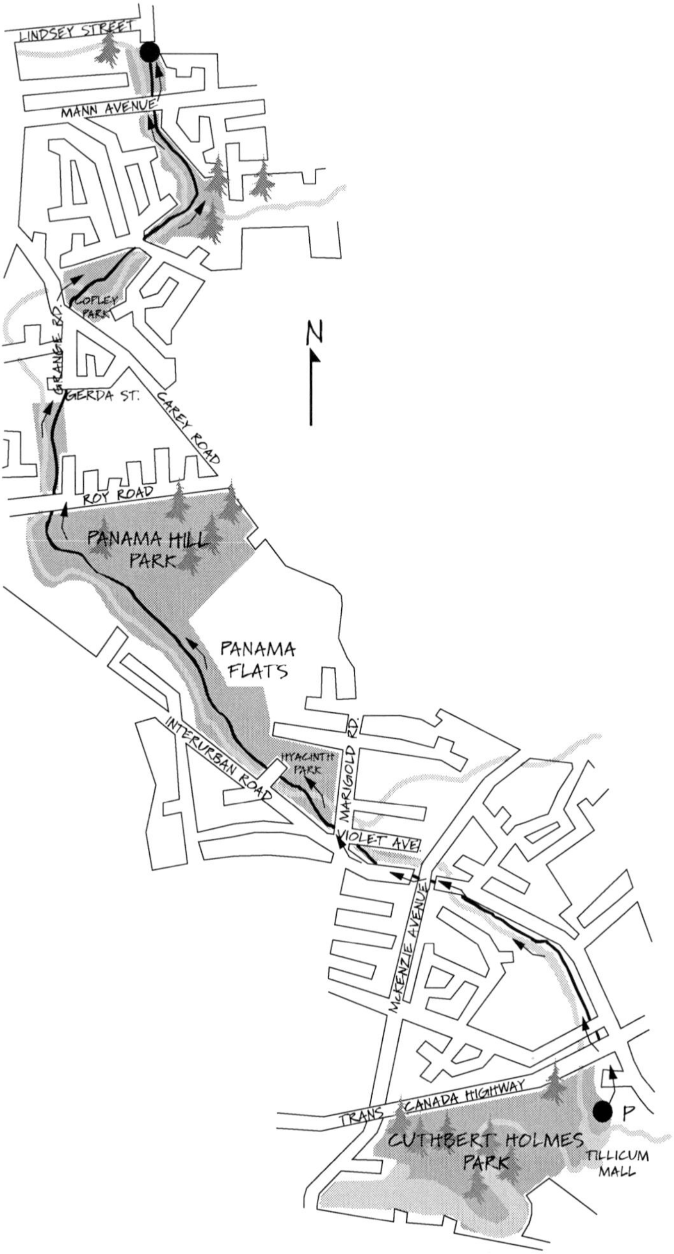

LINDSEY STREET

MANN AVENUE

COPLEY PARK

GRANGE RD.

GERDA ST.

CAREX ROAD

N

ROY ROAD

PANAMA HILL PARK

PANAMA FLATS

INTERURBAN ROAD

HYACINTH PARK

MARIGOLD RD.

VIOLET AVE.

McKENZIE AVENUE

TRANS CANADA HIGHWAY

P

CUTHBERT HOLMES PARK

TILLICUM MALL

There are two sections of boardwalk on the right bank of the creek and then, after 250 metres, a set of stepping stones to the left bank. Continue on for almost half a kilometre where the trail crosses to the left bank by both a bridge and a set of stepping stones. After a kilometre the trail passes under **McKenzie Avenue** and crosses **Interurban Road** to continue along a willow-lined section of the creek. Another 100 metres or so the trail crosses the narrow **Violet Avenue.** (This is the confluence of **Swan** and **Colquitz Creeks**.) Bear left on crossing Violet walking a few metres to meet and cross Marigold Road to enter **Hyacinth Park**. The trail now has the creek on the left.

After crossing a lane the trail becomes much wider and passes to the left of the expanse of **Panama Flats**, a large wetland area that is under cultivation during the dry season and attracts a wide variety of birds especially pheasant and quail. The trail rises slightly skirting the environmentally-sensitive **Panama Pond** and **Hill** — now called Panama Hill Park.

After a short descent the trail crosses Roy Road and then, after a further 150 metres, turns sharply right on **Gerda Road**. Walk about 30 metres along Gerda turning left on **Grange Road**. There is no trail here but after 200 metres, as Grange intersects Carey Road the trail resumes across the road at the narrow entrance to **Copley Park**.

Once in the park turn immediately right following the creek for 200 metres or so. Cross Vanalman Road to continue further into the park. Entering a wooded area the trail crosses the creek over a metal bridge and turns left to follow it. The trail soon turns left at a junction and, after passing a bridge to the left, crosses Mann Avenue. Two wooden bridges follow and then, after a short climb the trail meets and ends at **Lindsay Avenue**. (Saanich municipality plans to extend the trail along Lindsay to Wilkinson Road.)

(For an extension of this walk see also Walk 22 Quick's Bottom.) ●

15 CORDOVA RIDGE

It was the Spanish marine explorers who gave the name, Cordova, to the long, sweeping bay on the south-east shores of the Saanich peninsula. But the name of the ridge that rises sharply from the bay seems to have changed over the years.

To early settlers it was known as Rithet Hill (being part of R.P. Rithet's Broadmead Farm at that time), or Company Hill, then Bald Hill and later, after a reservoir was constructed in 1950, as Reservoir Hill. Today, it is simply known as Cordova Ridge and is home to hundreds of lucky residents many of whom have wonderful views of Haro Strait, San Juan Island and the mountains beyond.

Most of the ridge was logged in the early 1900s but second growth has returned some of the natural feeling of the place. One special example of this regenerated forest is Doumac Park.

Blending the first syllable of the names of two local real estate agents, Dougall and MacMorran for its name, this small two-and-a-half hectare piece of land is replete with ravine, creek, tall conifers and a long wooden stairway from ravine floor to a quiet residential cul-de-sac.

The park's creek, named, not unexpectedly, Doumac Creek, is covered with wire bales of rock which were installed as a preventive measure after a mudslide destroyed 10 metres of the downstream Lochside Drive in the winter of 1990.

Together with McMinn and Grant Parks, Doumac Park forms a nice forested interlude in what is essentially a residential walk.

General description

A loop walk through a delightful residential neighbourhood that includes four parks, a gradual climb to an enclosed reservoir and part of the Lochside Trail.

A profusion of ferns

Location
About 10 kilometres from downtown
Victoria on the south-east side of the
municipality of Saanich.

Length 2 hours

Level Easy to moderate

Special attractions
Lochside Drive (part of the Lochside
Trail system that terminates in
Sidney), one of Victoria's most pleas-
ant and treed residential streets;
Doumac Park with its ravine and tall
conifers; great easterly views of Haro
Strait, San Juan Island and on a clear
day, Mt. Baker.

How to get there
Follow Blanshard Street out of town
where it becomes the Pat Bay High-
way (#17). Take the Royal Oak Drive
exit and turn right onto Royal Oak
Drive. After almost two kilometres
and at the traffic light, turn left on
Lochside Drive. Follow Lochside for
half a kilometre parking opposite Sea
Ridge Drive at the beginning of
McMinn Park. *(Bus #32 Cordova
Bay.)*

CORDOVA RIDGE

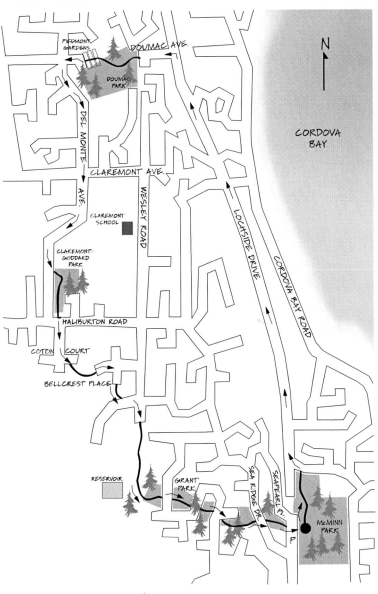

THE WALK   This walk begins at **McMinn Park**'s Lochside entrance opposite **Sea Ridge Drive**. Take this gravel path through the park keeping parallel to the Lochside Trail. After 200 metres or so exit the park at the top of Maplegrove Street and walk the short distance up to **Lochside Drive**. Continue on Lochside for a kilometre walking along one of Victoria's most pleasant suburban thoroughfares. You'll pass Haliburton Road, the recently created (2001) **Doris Page Park** and **Claremont Avenue** with its unimpeded expanse of ocean and San Juan Island views.

Shortly after Claremont you'll see, on your left the sign for **Doumac Park**. (The Doumac ravine plunges down to Cordova Bay Road on the right.) Follow the sign by walking up the short Doumac Avenue to the trailhead 40 metres on the left. This trail follows **Doumac Creek** through a mixed forest of cedar, fir, maple and alder for about 100 metres then forks right to climb to the flight of stairs up to **Piedmont Gardens**. At the top of the stairs turn right walking the short distance to **Del Monte Avenue**.

Turn left on Del Monte and, after crossing Claremont Avenue take the narrow path off Del Monte that leads to **Claremont-Goddard Park**. Walk through the park keeping parallel to Del Monte Avenue exiting onto **Haliburton Road**. Cross the road and walk up Haliburton Place immediately opposite. Turn left on **Coton Court** taking the 25 metre, narrow paved path that leads to **Bellcrest Place**. At Bellcrest take another narrow paved path to Wesley Court. Turn left here walking 30 metres to **Wesley Road**.

Turn right on Wesley and climb the fire access road to the **concrete reservoir** at the ridge's summit. (Pass through the fire gate part way up this road.) To the left and opposite the reservoir descend the ridge by a well-marked but very steep chip trail that forms the linear **Grant Park**. The trail crosses **Amblewood Drive** three times and Sea Ridge Drive once before terminating on Lochside Drive opposite McMinn Park. •

16 CUTHBERT HOLMES PARK

This small riverside park was officially opened in 1990. For such a compact area (27.4 hectares) the park embraces a number of distinct habitats from hedgerow and abandoned fields to mixed and conifer woodlands and river estuary. Named for Major H. Cuthbert Holmes, an advocate of preserving a greenbelt along the Colquitz Creek/River, the park exemplifies what can be done to protect wildlife habitat in the face of urban sprawl.

General description

A loop walk in an urban oasis set in the midst of a highway, a shopping mall and residential suburbia.

Location

Six kilometres out of town at the junction of the Trans-Canada Highway and Admirals Road.

Length

30 - 40 minute loop. (Possibility of extending the walk along the Colquitz River linear trail — Walk 14).

Level Easy

Special attractions

A rare opportunity to walk the banks of a local river near its estuary; a good interpretive sign.

How to get there

Take Douglas Street out of town and, as it becomes the divided Trans-Canada Highway, turn left at the second traffic light onto Admirals Road. After 100 metres, turn left again onto the park's access road and down to the carpark. *(Bus #21 Interurban. Access trail at Tillicum Mall).*

THE WALK From the **interpretive sign** at the carpark walk a few metres along the central, paved path and take a right turn onto a chip trail. Turn right again as the trail forks and then, after 20 metres or so, turn left onto the river trail. **Heron Bridge** is passed on the right and, after a long bend in the river, the trail joins the paved central trail. Turn right and follow the paved trail over a bridge and out of the woods into an open, hawthorn-bushed area.

CUTHBERT HOLMES PARK

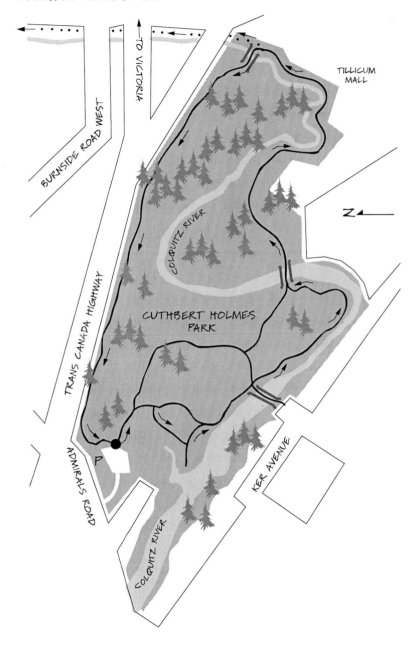

Tillicum Mall is straight ahead and a large movie house complex is on the right. The pavement becomes gravel as the trail curves close to the mall's parking lot. At about 50 metres before the highway overpass turn left over the creek on a concrete bridge taking the gravel path to the right until it meets the paved trail going left parallel to the highway. As the paved trail widens to a roadway curling up to **Admirals Road** take the short chip trail on the left down to the park's carpark.   •

· ·

17   ELK/BEAVER LAKE PARK (2 walks)

Established as a park by the Capital Regional District in 1966, Elk/Beaver has become one of the most accessible and used parks in the area. Once two separate lakes — Elk and Beaver — they have, over time become one. Only their names remain as a reminder of their singularity.

Encompassing over 411 hectares, the park accommodates a variety of habitats and activities. The lake and its surrounding wetlands attract many waterfowl including mergansers, buffleheads, mallards, Canada geese and loons. River otters, mink and bullfrogs frequent the shore. On the lake rowers, swimmers, anglers, windsurfers and water skiers all manage to share the surface in their designated areas. Although the trails in the park are primarily for walking there are those designated multi-use and allow horse-riding and cycling. On the park's eastern boundary open grassland offers dog lovers ample space to walk and train their dogs. In the park's forest dominated by Douglas-fir and western red cedar along with stands of cottonwoods and alders, bald eagles and osprey eye the lake for rainbow trout and bass.

There are two main beaches in the park — Beaver and Hamsterly — situated at the south and north ends of the lake respectively. These shallow waters and sandy beaches are ideal for swimming, picnicking and launching canoes for exploring offshore islands and the shoreline.

The park's western boundary is the vestigial Victoria and Sidney Line — an extinct railroad that between 1894 and 1919 travelled along the lake's twisting shoreline.

In this mixture of diverse natural environments and activities the walker becomes privy to some of the most pleasing surroundings Victoria has to offer.

General description

A main trail that loops around the lake. A shorter loop partly away from the water.

Location

12 kilometres north of downtown Victoria off the Patricia Bay Highway (Highway 17).

Length

Main trail: 2 – 2.5 hours
Short trail: 45 minutes

Level Easy

Special attractions

Lake views; forested trails; variety of waterfowl and birds; fishing platforms; beaches; vestiges of Victoria and Sidney Line railway.

How to get there

To the Beaver Lake carpark take Blanshard Street going north. Blanshard becomes Patricia Bay Highway (#17) at the outskirts of town. Follow the Royal Oak Drive exit after 8 kilometres. Turn left over the highway on Royal Oak Drive. After 200 metres turn right at the traffic light onto Elk Lake Drive. At one kilometre turn left into the entrance of Beaver Lake. Park at the first paved parking lot 200 metres along the driveway. *(Bus #70 Swartz Bay.)*

THE WALK: MAIN TRAIL The main trail loops completely around the lake and can be accessed at a number of points. For our purpose the trail head is situated at the end of the paved walkway down to the beach at **Beaver Lake**. At the beach turn left and walk the trail clockwise. Cross the narrow metal footbridge over **Colquitz Creek** after 200 metres. Between this point and one kilometre from the start, there are a number of intersecting trails. Ignore them, taking only the trail that keeps the lake on your right.

After a narrow, winding section, the trail joins a wider trail that was originally the **Victoria and Sidney Line railway**. This wide trail offers expansive views across the lake and is a good vantage point to watch the rowers scudding across the water. At four kilometres the trail, after passing a **fishing platform**, becomes a **paved road**. Leave the road 200 metres along the pavement on a trail that dips down to the right through a small carpark. The trail continues through the trees and becomes undulating and twisty. A wooden bridge at five kilometres crosses **O'Donnel Creek** as the trail continues past numerous lake accesses toward **Hamsterly Beach**. Amenities at Hamsterly include toilets, water, and in the summer months, snacks.

The trail beyond the beach squeezes between the lake and highway until, at the **boat houses**, it veers west. After a picnic shelter in the trees on the right the trail branches. One trail going close to the lake, the other a straight path along **open grass land**. Keep to the straight path if you don't want to add another kilometre to your walk. At the end of the straight section the trail moves into a treed area and winds closer to the lake. Again, keep the lake close to your right. You know you're getting close to the Beaver Lake beach and parking lot when the trail begins to hug the shoreline.

JAMES R. SMITH

SHORT TRAIL From the Beaver Lake parking lot walk down the paved walkway to the lake. Turn left on the gravel trail and follow the lake over a **narrow metal bridge**. A hundred metres after the bridge the trail turns abruptly to the right to follow the lake. At this point turn left and follow a trail that rises through the trees behind the

ELK / BEAVER LAKE PARK

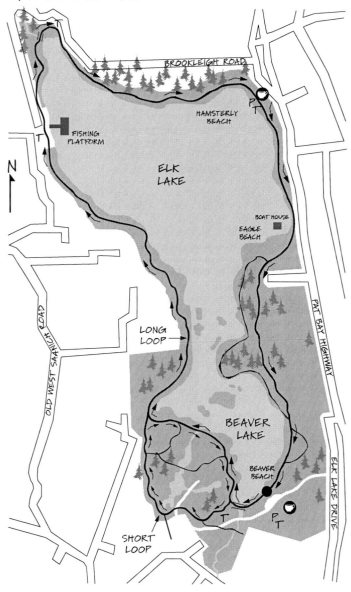

picnic area. This trail soon intersects another trail from the left (the **Pipeline Trail**).

Turn right at this junction and continue until this trail meets the wide, former railroad bed trail. Keep to the right and follow this wide trail for almost half a kilometre until the lake comes into view. Turn right just before the lake down a short pitch on a trail marked "**To Beaver Lake**". From this point keep the lake on the left. The trail meanders along the shoreline back to the parking lot.

For shorter walks a walker can simply walk in either direction from the Beaver Lake beach for an out-and-back walk. •

. . . .

18 FRANCIS/KING REGIONAL PARK (3 walks)

Originally two separate parks, the 113-hectare Francis/King Park was formed in 1981 by the Capital Regional District from the Thomas Francis and the Freeman King Parks. The land for the Thomas Francis Park was the legacy of the Francis family — early pioneers of the area. First purchased by James Francis in the 1840s and left to his son Thomas, the land was largely intact when it was bequeathed to the province by Thomas in 1960. The land west of Munns Road *came into the city's hands in 1967 and was given the name Freeman King Park in memory of Freeman King a respected early conservationist and naturalist.*

General Description
A mostly-forested park with century-old Douglas-fir and western red cedar trees. A profusion of wildflowers in spring gives an added pleasure to walking.

Location
13 kilometres west of downtown not far off the Trans-Canada Highway.

Trail marker in Francis/King Regional Park

Length

Centennial Trail: 50 minutes
High Ridge Trail: 40 minutes
**Centennial/High Ridge Trails
combined**: 1.5 hours

Level Easy to moderate.

Special attractions

Forest trails; abundance of wildflowers especially shooting star; nature house; some grassy bolds; boardwalk nature trail; tall-tree grove.

How to get there

Take Douglas Street/Trans-Canada Highway out of town. After eight kilometres take the Helmcken (Hospital) off ramp. Turn right on Helmcken then turn left onto Burnside Road West. After a kilometre turn right onto Prospect Lake Road. Turn left on Munns Road. Francis/King Park carpark and Nature House are located 100 metres on the right.

THE WALK: CENTENNIAL TRAIL The trailhead is located between the **Nature House** and the adjacent **Forester's Cabin**. For the most part this is a steadily-undulating trail with only the occasional steep descent. Signage for the trail is very clear and adequate. However, at the first junction with the **Grand Fir Trail** you must bear right and cross **Munns Road** about 100 metres north of the Grand Fir

FRANCIS/KING PARK

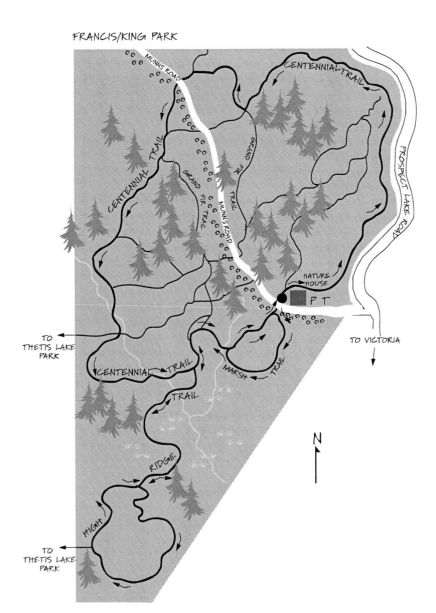

TO
THETIS LAKE
PARK

TO VICTORIA

TO
THETIS LAKE
PARK

N

Trail crossing. A bridle path which runs parallel with Munns Road must be crossed to continue along the **Centennial Trail**.

A short distance after the road crossing be aware of the trail's second intersection with Grand Fir Trail, there the two trails are the same route for 50 odd metres before the **Grand Fir** veers sharply left. At the southern extremity of the trail the terrain becomes less forested and more gladed. Watch for a trail going off to the right. This is one of three trails that link Francis/King with the much larger **Thetis Lake Park**. The trail now swings east until its junction with **High Ridge Trail**. Turn left here and follow the signs marked Nature House to complete the hike.

For a longer and more hilly hike turn right at the High Ridge/ Centennial junction and follow the ridge trail south. (Follow the instruction below marked*****.)

HIGH RIDGE TRAIL (This trail can be accessed only via the Centennial Trail.) From the park's carpark cross **Munns Road** to the trailhead and turn left on the marked **Marsh Trail**. The trail descends for 70 metres into a grove of cedars and a swampy area. After going through a clump of alders the trail rises gently to join the **Centennial Trail**. Turn left to follow this trail. You soon cross a short wooden bridge and then turn left at a trail junction.

*At the next trail junction turn left again on the trail marked **High Ridge**. The trail soon rises to gain the ridge and, at the next junction (both trails marked High Ridge) take the left fork. On the ridge the terrain becomes undulating and the trees less dense.

At the southern reaches of the park the trail hugs the fence line for some time before turning north to climb steeply back onto the ridge. Pass the **Thetis Lake Park** trail on the left and continue back to complete this southern loop. Turn left at the trail junction and then on past the junction with Centennial to follow the signs marked **Nature House** back to the trailhead. •

21 KNOCKAN HILL PARK

Walking up the gradual hill through tall firs and craggy Garry oaks to the moss and grass-covered rocks at its top, it's easy to understand why the Songhees First Nation might have called Knockan Hill "Nga'k'un" meaning "rocks on top". Or why, in the 1850s, Scottish settlers might have referred to the place in their native gaelic as "Gnocan" meaning a hill or knob. No matter how it got its name this 8-hectare park has been used for almost a century as an ideal spot for walks, picnics and a place to observe nature in a very tranquil setting.

At the main entrance to the park stands Stranton Lodge — an English arts and crafts-style house once owned by the late Tom and Maude Hall. In 1973 Maude Hall sold the property to the Saanich municipality and in the early nineties it was designated by the Saanich Heritage Foundation as a heritage site.

General description
An out-and-back wooded and slightly hilly trail to a Garry oak, grass and rock outcropping.

Location
On the border between View Royal and Saanich municipalities about seven kilometres north-west of downtown Victoria off Burnside Road West.

Length 30 minutes out-and-back. 45 minutes including a loop.

Level Easy

Special attractions
Garry oaks and rock outcroppings; heritage buildings; wildflowers and birds.

How to get there
Take Douglas Street to the Trans-Canada Highway out of town. After the intersection of Tillicum and Mackenzie take the next exit at Helmcken Road (signed for the hospital). Half a kilometre along Helmcken, turn right at the lighted Burnside Road West. Turn left after two blocks onto High Street. Park on the right side of road just before the Strawberry Vale Community Hall. *(Bus #22 Burnside.)*

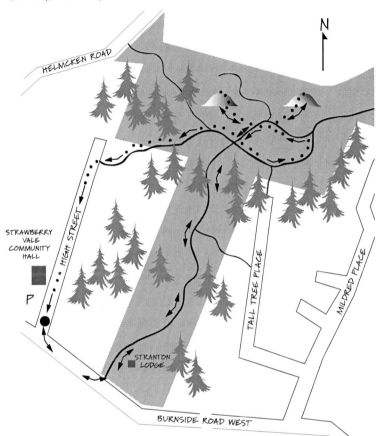

THE WALK From the parking area on **High Street** turn left on **Burnside Road West** walking the 50 metres to the signed entrance to the park (Burnside is a busy road so please keep well to the roadside). Walk up the trail which is also the driveway to the heritage-designated **Stranton Lodge**, once the home of Tom and Maude Hall. Continue on the well-defined out-and-back trail as it winds up to the summit through grand firs, broadleaf maples, Garry oaks and moss-covered rock out-croppings. The trail terminates just before the rocks of the east and west viewpoints. Retrace the trail back to Burnside.

For a **loop course** turn right just before the viewpoints on a **chip trail**. Keep left at a trail junction and take the next left trail up to the viewpoint. There is no discernable trail between the east and west viewpoints. To descend, take the **gravel trail** immediately below the viewpoints walking down to the first trail junction. Two tall **Douglas-fir** trees mark this spot. Take the right chip trail, following it until it intersects a fire road at a metal trail marker. Turn right on the fire road walking 40 or 50 metres down to the roadway of **High Street**. Turn left on High Street walking down to the carpark at the community hall. •

. . . .

19   LAYRITZ, LOGAN & TREVLAC PARKS (3 walks)

Surrounded by hobby farms, stables and horses, chicken runs and the occasional llama, the three parks of Layritz, Logan and Trevlac are examples of what Saanich municipality does admirably — preserving beautiful and diverse lands for the enjoyment of its residents and visitors.

All three parks are named after long-time area residents who either gave or sold part of their properties to the municipality.

It was in 1952 that Richard Layritz, owner of a large parcel

of land west of Wilkinson Road, offered a 4.5-hectare portion for a park. Eleven years later, after Layritz's death, his wife gifted a further 2.25 hectares as a memorial to her husband. A year later, in 1964, Mr. DeWilde, the owner of Layritz Nurseries Ltd., a company Richard Layritz had started, offered to sell an additional 11 hectares from the nursery's land to the municipality.

Logan Park is the oldest of the three parks, being established in 1925 after it was acquired from Edward Logan. Logan was one of the early settlers in the area, previously known as the Burnside Park subdivision. Since 1914 he had been trying to negotiate with Saanich for the municipality to build a road from the then shorter Viaduct Avenue through his property to Prospect Lake Road. He had offered just over 12 hectares for a park if they would build the road. The exchange didn't happen although, fortunately for us, the municipality did agree years later to purchase 6.5 hectares of his land for use as a park and to name it after him.

In the early 1970s Giff (Gilbert) Calvert began transforming his 8 hectare piece of land along Prospect Lake Road into a nature sanctuary. Over many years he created and nurtured an extensive wetland and pond area. The pond is stocked with trout and the surrounding wetland is rich with waterfowl and wetland flora. With its accompanying rock outcroppings and conifer forest the land was a perfect site for the municipality to purchase when it was offered in 1988. The name Trevlac is

simply Giff's surname, Calvert, spelt backwards.

General description
A loop walk on the outskirts of Victoria in an area that is decidedly rural in flavour. You walk through a wide meadow, beside two ponds and along quiet roads. Two shorter loops are options.

Location
Eight kilometres from the city centre in the Interurban area of the Saanich municipality.

Length
Long loop: 2.5 hours.
Medium loop: 1.5 hours.
Short loop: 30 – 45 minutes.

Level Easy to moderate.

Special attraction
Two wetland areas with year-round ponds (great for birding); rural roads; two small parks in the heart of a rural Douglas-fir woodland; a little-explored area of the Saanich municipality.

How to get there
Take Blanshard Street and then the Pat Bay Highway to the Quadra Street exit. Turn left over the highway and then left onto Glanford Avenue. Turn right onto Mann Avenue and after the lights at Mann and Wilkinson, park on the left side of the no-exit part of Mann. *(Bus #31 Glanford)*

LAYRITZ/LOGAN/TREVLAC PARKS

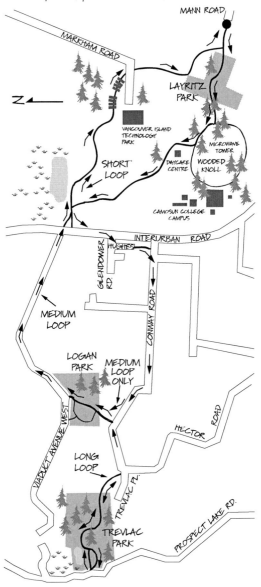

THE WALK   From the Mann Road entrance follow the paved path into **Layritz Park**. Walk through the baseball diamonds to the wooded lands on the west side of the park. Turn right along the circular gravel path and right again in front of the daycare centre. Cross the roadway to walk through a **grassy meadow**. The trail veers left to travel along the wooded border of the meadow down to the pond of the **Horticultural Centre of the Pacific**. Continue past a trail junction keeping to your left. (Notice the observatory at the Centre of the Universe on the hilltop straight ahead.) For a shorter walk (short loop) turn right here following the trail back to Layritz Park. (See description at * below.)

The trail enters the woods for a short distance before emerging onto **Interurban Road**. Turn left on Interurban and walk 200 metres to **Hughes Road** on the right. (This is also signed for **Glendower** and **Densmore**.) Turn left on Hughes and after the roadway ends follow the wide trail that joins **Conway Road** at which point you turn right. Conway is a rather undulating and rural road — very pleasant to walk.

After a kilometre there is a sharp right turn as Conway becomes **Hector Road**. You'll pass the entrance to **Logan Park** on your right (for the medium loop turn right here and follow the description at ** below) and then at **Trevlac Place** at the signed Calvert Park you turn sharp right and then right again into Trevlac (Calvert) Park itself.

The trail through the park is rough but well-defined. It soon rises to a bluff and then follows the eastern edge of the park down a gentle slope. The trail then traverses the park and enters a small but dense **cedar grove** in the middle of which is a **trail marker**. Turn left here and at the next marker turn right. After about 50 or 60 metres you'll notice a bench to your right overlooking the park's main feature — **a wetland area**. (If you're a birder this is a great place to get your binocs out.) The path widens as it draws close to its exit onto **Prospect Lake Road**.

From the road, retrace your steps taking the trail about 75 metres on the left. This leads down to the wetland area. At the next trail junction turn right along a bumpy, windy trail heading back to the cedar grove and the trail marker. Turn left here following the path back to Trevlac

Llamas on Viaduct Avenue West

Place and Hector Road. At Hector turn left and walk back to the **Logan Park entrance**.

** Turn left here and, always keeping to your right, walk through this wooded park to **Viaduct Avenue West**. Turn right on Viaduct walking along this delightful, but hilly road back to **Interurban Road**. At Interurban cross the road and walk a few metres to the right to descend down a narrow trail into a wooded area overlooking wetland and the pond of the Horticultural Centre of the Pacific. This rough trail soon intersects a good gravel trail on which you turn left. This trail very quickly meets a chip trail — which you take ignoring the trail to your right.

*Turn right after about 40 metres as the trail follows a wooded border of the wide meadow. The trail bears left into the woods and descends to another junction. Take the trail going right and just before the **Vancouver Island Technology Park** buildings, the trail turns left to enter the woods once again. There follows a wetish section with two wooden bridges before the trail exits onto **Markham Road**. Cross the road and turn right along a paved driveway and then into a chip trail back into **Layritz Park**. Follow this trail to the paved path and turn left walking the short distance back to the Mann Road entrance. •

20 MOUNT DOUGLAS PARK (2 walks)

Mount Doug, as it's known locally, is probably the closest thing to a wilderness experience a person can have just minutes away from the city.

Originally known as Cedar Hill, Mount Douglas was renamed after Sir James Douglas, the first governor of British Columbia. Back in 1858, Douglas, recognizing the beauty and importance of the area, established the park as a protected reserve. The park's extensive trail system, many of which bear the names of early settlers and farms, take the visitor through dense forest and up to the 227-metre summit for spectacular views of the city, the peninsula, mountains and ocean. Part of the park borders the southern shore of Cordova Bay. Above a sandy beach is a picnic and play area. The trail down to the shore follows Douglas Creek as it drains into the bay.

General description
Two walks in the largest park of the Saanich park system. One to the summit, the other around the perimeter.

Location
Twelve kilometres north of the city's centre in the municipality of Saanich.

Length
Summit loop: 1 – 1.5 hours.
Perimeter loop: 1 – 1.5 hours.

Level
Summit loop: Moderate to strenuous.
Perimeter loop: Easy to moderate.

Special attraction
The summit's elevation of 227 metres gives spectacular 360-degree views of the Saanich peninsula, the city, the ocean and mountains (including Mount Baker on a clear day); dense fir, cedar, maple and Garry oak forest (the largest urban forest in the region) surrounds the rocky peak; a good example of a monadnock — an isolated hill that has resisted the erosive forces of millennia; picnic tables and beach access on the park's eastern boundary.

How to get there
Follow Blanshard out of town as

it becomes the Pat Bay Highway (#17). At eight kilometres take the Royal Oak Drive exit. Turn right on Royal Oak and, at the third traffic light, cross the intersection to continue on Cordova Bay Road.

After a further one and half kilometres turn left (just before Ash Road) into the Mount Douglas Park carpark. *(Bus #39 UVic or Royal Roads.)*

THE WALK: SUMMIT LOOP The trailhead is on the right of the **interpretive sign** on the west side of the carpark. The trail rises through the trees to **Cordova Bay Road**. Cross the road turning right a few metres into the trees on the **Whittaker Trail**. The trail winds and gently undulates parallel to the road and just past a grassy opening, rises sharply to the left to a trail junction.

Take the unmarked **Merriman Trail** going up and slightly to the left. After about 50 metres the Merriman crosses the **Norn Trail** and continues as a narrow, uneven trail winding upwards. At the next trail junction turn left onto the very narrow and unmarked **Irvine Trail**. This trail soon climbs steeply to the park road **(Churchill Drive)**. Cross the road walking to the right and, after 30 metres, turn left onto the continuation of the marked Irvine Trail. Keep to this well-worn, wandering trail as it climbs, almost always to the right, toward the summit.

The closer to the summit the more steeply pitched and rocky the trail becomes. Climb the stair-like rocks up to the summit radio mast on the left and then descend briefly to cross the carpark and onto the well marked trail to the summit's viewing platform.

Commence the descent by taking the short flight of stairs to the left of the protruding carpark and viewing area. This is the **Glendenning Trail**, a very narrow, rocky trail, that descends in a south-westerly direction. After an extensive slump area turn left at a trail junction onto the wide **Whittaker Trail**.

At the next junction turn left walking down the unmarked Whittaker Trail that soon widens into a fire road. A few metres before the fire gate turn left along Whittaker as it parallels **Cedar Hill Road**. Cross the

MOUNT DOUGLAS PARK

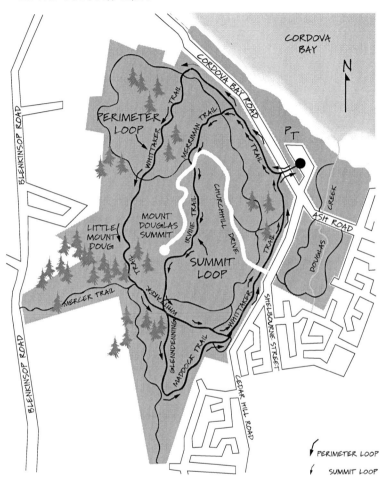

summit road continuing along the **Whittaker Trail** for a few hundred metres before crossing Cordova Bay Road back to the carpark.

THE WALK: PERIMETER LOOP The trail begins, as with the Summit loop, to the right of the **interpretive sign** of the park's carpark. Walk to the road, cross it and follow the **Whittaker Trail** to the right as it winds and undulates parallel to **Cordova Bay Road**. Just past an open grassy area the trail rises sharply to the left for a few metres to a trail junction. (There is a fire hydrant located here.) Continue to the right keeping to the main trail until, at 300 metres, it turns abruptly left. After a few metres it turns left again onto a wider trail coming from the right. Bear right as the trail begins to narrow to become a rocky and rooted but well-worn track through the forest.

Follow the trail as it ascends steeply to the left and then swings right ignoring a trail off to the left. There soon follows another trail junction. Take the well-used trail to the right. (Throughout this walk, the summit of Mount Douglas will always be on the left.) The trail swings left as it follows the contours of the mount and, after a few hundred metres, passes between Mount Douglas and **Little Mount Douglas**. Ignore trails to the right that climb to the smaller summit. The trail becomes wide for a brief moment before descending to a trail junction at the remains of a mine shaft. Follow the trail straight ahead between four tall fir trees. The trail soon passes the **Mercer Trail** marker as it continues to the significant trail junction of the **Glendenning, Whittaker** and **Harrop Trails**. Take the unmarked but wide Glendenning Trail that descends to the right. Ignore two narrow trails on the left before, at about 500 metres, taking the wider **Maddock Trail** (unmarked) to the left. This trail soon joins a gravel road that descends to **Cedar Hill Road**.

At this road turn left and left again through a fire gate to join the **Whittaker Tail** going to the right paralleling the road. Cross the park's **Churchill Drive** (the summit road) and follow the trail to the trail marker and, crossing Cordova Bay Road, walk back to the parking lot. •

22 QUICK'S BOTTOM

Sounding rather like something out of a Shakespearean comedy, Quick's Bottom refers not to someone's rear end but to an actual person and a landform. William Quick was a Saanich farmer who was renowned for having the first herd of purebred Jersey milk cows on Vancouver Island. Bottom refers, as one might suspect, to bottom or marshland. The marshland situated west of Wilkinson Road and south of West Saanich Road was part of William Quick's farm and was thus named Quick's Bottom.

The marshland is one of the few remaining in the Victoria area and it was in 1976 that the Saanich municipality, recognizing its importance, preserved it as a wildlife sanctuary.

General description

An easy, short trail on the outskirts of town through predominantly marsh-land. Out-and-back with a loop. (No dogs.)

Location

Ten kilometres north of the city centre in a semi-rural area of Saanich.

Length 30 – 40 minutes.

Level Easy

Special attractions

Bird blind — a viewing platform which conceals the viewer — located above the marsh; wide variety of wildlife including waterfowl, song birds, bald eagles and muskrats; profusion of cat-tails and English hawthorn bushes.

How to get there

Take Blanshard Street out of town where it becomes the Pat Bay Highway. After eight kilometres take the Royal Oak Drive exit. Turn left on Royal Oak driving over the highway, past the lights at Elk Lake Drive and at West Saanich Road and Wilkinson Road. Continue along Wilkinson for half a kilometre turning left onto Greenlea Drive. Use this road for parking. *(Bus #30 Carey Road.)*

THE WALK   From Greenlea Drive walk back to Wilkinson Road and turn left. (The house on the hill slightly to the left across Wilkinson Road is the original **Quick's farmhouse** and dates back to 1912.) Keeping to the left hand sidewalk, walk 150 metres before crossing **Wilkinson** at the **Quick's Bottom trail sign**. The trail proper begins five metres off the road and drops 60 metres to a wooden bridge spanning **Colquitz Creek**.

Over the bridge the trail twists and turns through a maze of hawthorn bushes and small trees for a few hundred metres always keeping the marsh on the right and farmland on the left. Watch for and take the trail going to the right. This is the beginning of the loop section of the trail and immediately crosses a small stream on a wooden bridge before heading for the **bird blind** — 100 metres on the left. There are generous views of the open marshland from this point and, in winter, patches of open water can be seen in the middle of the marsh.

The trail climbs briefly to a shoulder of the marsh and quickly drops before taking a sharp turn up to **Markham Road**. Turn left on the paved Markham walking past the **Saanich Park's nursery** 100 or so metres along the road. Just past the nursery a trail marker points the direction to the left. Take this chip trail back to Wilkinson Road.

At Wilkinson, cross the road immediately opposite the Quick's

JAMES R. SMITH

Quick's Bottom bird blind

Bottom sign taking the trail that leads between the houses. This is a short trail but will save walking back to Greenlea via the busy Wilkinson. After 40 metres the chip ends and a paved path continues to the left for another 30 metres emerging onto **Viaduct Avenue East**. Turn left on Viaduct and then right or left on Greenlea depending on where your car is parked. •

QUICK'S BOTTOM

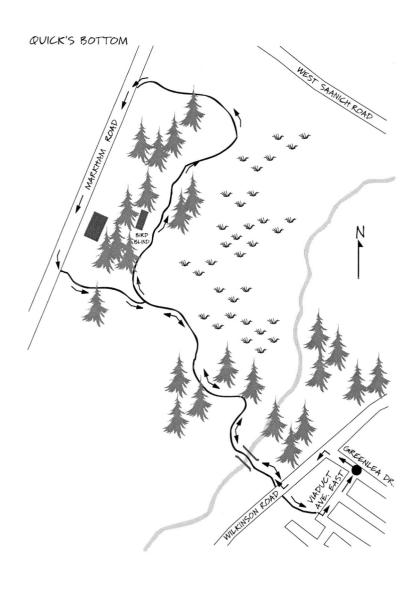

23 RITHET'S BOG

R.P. Rithet was a Scottish immigrant who became a very successful and wealthy businessman in Victoria during the late 1800s. Although he and his family lived in high style in Victoria, he owned a 295-hectare farm named Broadmead Farm near Royal Oak on the Saanich Road. The bog which bears his name was part of the farmland and is now preserved as a 42-hectare nature sanctuary. The almost three kilometre trail that circles the bog passes through habitats that are typical of the southern island, i.e. Douglas-fir and Garry oak forests, rocky outcrops, swamp and meadow. It is also home to a variety of wildlife including lizards, birds, fish and muskrats.

General description

A short, mainly chip and gravel loop trail around Rithet's Bog in the heart of suburban Broadmead. (No dogs.)

Location

Five kilometres north of the city off the Pat Bay Highway.

Length 30 minutes

Level Easy

Special attractions

Abundant wildlife habitat; easy access and a flat terrain; viewing platform at the north end (Dalewood Lane).

How to get there

Leave town on Blanshard Street. At the edge of town Blanshard becomes the Pat Bay Highway (#17). Take the Quadra Street exit at about six kilometres. Turn right on Quadra and then immediately left at the traffic lights onto Chatterton Way. On the left 30 metres past the intersection of Chatterton and Emily Carr Drive are parking lots for office buildings. Park here. The trail is accessed directly opposite the entrance to the first parking lot. *(Bus #6 Quadra.)*

THE WALK Access the trail via the short path at the **bus stop** opposite the Broadmead office building complex (Cedar Building) on **Chatterton Way**.

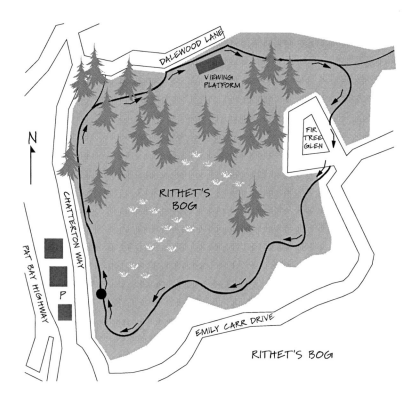

RITHET'S BOG

Turn right on the trail walking the circular route clockwise i.e. always keeping the bog on the right. After 700 metres the trail rises sharply to the left to join **Dalewood Lane**. Turn right on Dalewood and walk on the asphalt sidewalk passing a wooden sheltered **viewing platform** on the right. At 150 metres the sidewalk descends on a gravel path to the trail below which continues through a dense bushy area for 50 metres. The bush gives way to a mixed forest dominated by tall Douglas-fir.

The trail forks at a large boulder on the right at the far end of the forest. Take the right fork and cross the **wooden bridge** over a shallow creek. Another 10 metres and the trail joins a residential street (**Fir Tree Glen**). Turn left along the street for a 100 metres and then, at the trail marker on the right, continue along the well-maintained chip and gravel trail. Along the southern edge of the bog the trail undulates on a wider trail before passing a low rocky outcrop on the right. The trail ends after a long curve at the south-east end of the bog. •

24 SWAN LAKE/CHRISTMAS HILL NATURE SANCTUARY (2 walks)

Not far from the hustle of downtown lie the secluded hectares of the Swan Lake/Christmas Hill Nature Sanctuary.

As the words "lake" and "hill" imply, there are two very distinct environments encompassed within the sanctuary. The lake and its surrounding wetlands are a natural habitat for a variety of waterfowl while the surrounding trees and hedgerows provide homes for nesting sparrows, wrens and finches. Mink, muskrat and river otter live year round in the rocky portions of the lake shore.

By contrast, the highland landscape of Christmas Hill, which reaches an elevation of 122 metres is dominated by rocky outcrops, a Garry oak forest and a profusion of wildflowers and is home to song birds in the spring and summer.

Together, these two differing natural worlds give the visitor an opportunity, in a short space of time, to connect with a variety of nature's offerings both flora and fauna.

General description
Swan Lake — a mostly lakeside trail offering sightings of birds and shoreline animals. **Christmas Hill** — a modest uphill trail. (No dogs.)

Location
Five kilometres north of downtown Victoria.

Length
Swan Lake: 40 – 45 minutes
Christmas Hill: 30 minutes uphill, 20 minutes down

Level
Swan Lake: easy
Christmas Hill: easy to moderate.

Special attractions
Swan Lake: nature house; nature walks; boardwalks; bird-watching. Christmas Hill: summit view of the city and surrounding hills and islands; rocky outcrops; Garry oak forest.

How to get there
From downtown take Blanshard Street which becomes the Pat Bay Highway for five kilometres and take the McKenzie Avenue exit

A swan, of course, on the shore of Swan Lake

right. Turn right again almost immediately on Rainbow Street. Ignore the "no-exit" signs on Rainbow and continue straight until the street intersects Ralph Street. (There is a sanctuary sign here) Turn left on Ralph. The carpark for the sanctuary is situated at the end of the street. *(Bus #26 UVic.)*

NOTE: To return to downtown follow in reverse the above directions back to McKenzie Avenue. Turn right onto McKenzie and then right at the second set of traffic lights onto Saanich Road. Continue along Saanich Road to the lights at Blanshard Street. Turn left onto Blanshard.

SWAN LAKE: THE WALK From the carpark take the path to the left of the **Nature House**. Continue left down a rocky path to the shoreline trail. Turn left again along a paved path for 20 metres then right on the chip trail. Turn right at the trail marked "**Loop Trail**." Avoid the Christmas Hill trail sign keeping the lake to the right. Pass over a few short boardwalks through a thick bushy and marshy area. After 500 metres the path winds closer to the lake and passes through a grove of Garry oaks. Through the trees there are unimpeded views of the marsh with the lake in the distance.

At about the one kilometre mark the trail crosses the **Blenkinsop Creek** and on through a small meadow. Beyond the meadow the trail

SWAN LAKE / CHRISTMAS HILL

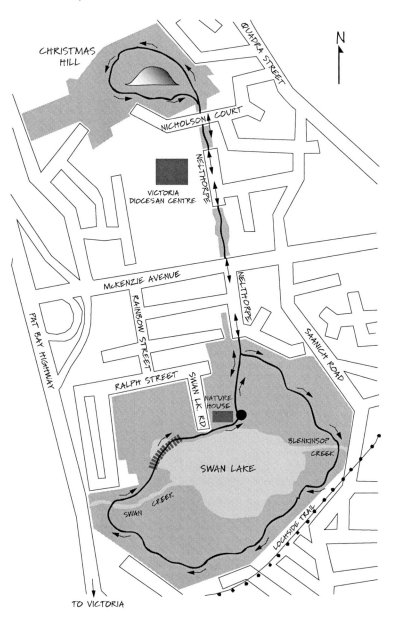

CHRISTMAS HILL

QUADRA STREET

N

NICHOLSON COURT

NELTHORPE

VICTORIA
DIOCESAN CENTRE

McKENZIE AVENUE

NELTHORPE

RAINBOW STREET

PAT BAY HIGHWAY

SAANICH ROAD

RALPH STREET

SWAN LK. RD.

NATURE
HOUSE

BLENKINSOP
CREEK

SWAN LAKE

SWAN CREEK

LOCHSIDE TRAIL

TO VICTORIA

descends through a stand of Garry oaks, maple and alder trees to a rocky portion of the trail very close to the lake shore. After a 150 metres the trail passes a **boardwalk** and **viewing platform** on the right. Continue straight through another meadow bordering an extensive marshy area. A line of cottonwood trees obscures the lake at this point but at the top of a short rise the lake comes back into view with the Nature House on the far shore and Christmas Hill beyond rising above a cluster of houses.

The trail gently undulates for almost a kilometre along the lake's marshy edge until, after a long curve, it enters a thick bushy area. Shortly, the trail crosses **Swan Lake Creek** via a bridge and then forks. Take the right fork along a gravel section of the trail. On reaching the open waters of the lake there begins a long, **90 metre floating boardwalk** over its western end. There are two benches situated on the boardwalk for viewing waterfowl and taking in the whole extent of the lake. The boardwalk continues on a winding course for another 30 to 40 metres before ending a short distance from the **Nature House**. Walk up the stone steps to pass in front of the building and then turn left to reach the carpark.

CHRISTMAS HILL: THE WALK From the northeast corner of the sanctuary parking lot (opposite exit) follow the path a short distance to the left until it forks. Take the left fork marked "**Christmas Hill**". After about 50 metres the trail crosses a small meadow to Nelthorpe, a residential street. Walk up the street to its junction with **McKenzie Avenue**. Cross McKenzie at the light-controlled pedestrian crossing. The trail continues directly across from **Nelthorpe Street** following a sharp but short ascent through a wooded area and is well marked as it gradually nears the hill. At 100 metres the trail joins the continuation of Nelthorpe Street and follows this steep road for 50 metres before entering the woods. To the left is the attractive woodland setting of the **Victoria Diocesan Pastoral Centre**.

The trail crosses Nicholson Street where a flight of stairs leads into an impressive stand of Douglas-fir. The next 50 or so metres are a steep ascent into the **Christmas Hill sanctuary** proper. The summit can be circumnavigated in either direction. The suggested route here is counter-clockwise climbing to summit viewpoint on the hill's north-west side. Descend via the lake viewpoint on the hill's south side. Continue around the summit trail to join the out-and-back trail to the Swan Lake carpark. •

. . . .

25 TEN MILE POINT

Over one and a half centuries ago, in 1843, an English brigantine sailed into the sheltered waters of a bay that was soon to bear the vessel's name — Cadboro. At the time Cadboro Bay was the home of the Songhees First Nation before they moved a few years later to Victoria's Inner Harbour. The Songhees were followed by the first white settlers in the bay — farm hands who worked at the nearby 445-hectare Uplands Farm.

East of Cadboro Bay is the imposing peninsula of Ten Mile Point — an area of land named for being ten nautical miles from Esquimalt Harbour. This piece of land has a surprising and rather bizarre history. Believe it or not, Telegraph Cove on the east side of the point was once the site of a dynamite manufacturing company — the Giant Powder Company. From the mid to late 1800s dynamite (used for mining and road construction on the mainland) had been shipped to Ten Mile Point from the company's California plant. But in 1895 the company, sensing a growing need for its product, moved operations to Telegraph Cove and actually manufactured the *dynamite there.*

Around the same time some enterprising Victoria business-men, seeing the potential of such a scenic area, drew plans for a large subdivision called Cadboro Bay Park Estate. This plan was never fully realized and for almost 80 years houses were built sporadically on the point. The most recent land development of the point has been that of Minnie Mountain, its highest part. The mountain was, until the early 1980s, only accessible by foot. Today it is completely developed with the grand name of Wedgewood Estates.

General Description

A walk encompassing: a sandy beach; woodland trails; rock out-croppings; ocean views; streets that are among the most pleasant in the area.

Location

Seven kilometres northeast of the city in the neighbourhood of Cadboro Bay.

Length 2 hours

Level Moderate

Special attractions

Varied terrain; great views from the Phyllis Park lookout (Haro Strait, Mount Baker, the San Juan Islands); picnic on a sandy beach; refreshments at Olive Olio's Café or the Smuggler's Cove Pub — both in Cadboro Bay village.

How to get there

Take the one-way Fort Street out of town crossing Oak Bay Avenue, Richmond Road and Foul Bay Road. After Foul Bay Road, Fort Street becomes Cadboro Bay Road. The road passes the Uplands Golf Course on the left and then descends into Cadboro Bay Village. Just before the village turn right at the four-way stop sign at the bottom of the hill onto Sinclair Road. Sinclair runs directly into the parking lot for Cadboro Bay's Gyro Park. *(Bus #11 Uplands.)*

THE WALK   From the **Gyro Park** parking lot walk to the beach. To the right is the **Royal Victoria Yacht Club**; to the left **Ten Mile Point** and **Discovery Island** beyond. Walk to the left along the beach exiting onto a road 50 metres before the bluffs at the end of the beach. (If the tide is too high to safely walk the beach, take the footpath to the left of the toilets and walk to Cadboro Bay Road. Turn right and walk to the just described point.)

From the beach walk the road for 10 metres and turn right on Tudor Avenue at the no-exit sign. There is a steep but short path here that leads to the continuation of **Tudor Road**. Turn right at the top of the path taking **Seaview Road** which curves along the shoreline with homes and gardens on both sides of the road. After a kilometre and opposite **Cadboro Bay View Road** take the signed footpath on the left that climbs up through the trees to **Tudor Avenue**.

At Tudor turn right and, crossing the road, walk 200 metres to **Bedford Road**. Turn left on Bedford. Take the path on the left as Bedford turns sharply right to become **Sea Point Drive**. (You are now on the edge of **Konukson Park**.) Follow this path past two intersecting paths bearing always to the left. The path now gains ground for a few hundred metres before it ends on the narrow paved upper section of **Phyllis Road**.

Turn right on Phyllis passing through a fireroad barrier. Ten metres past the barrier take the marked path on the left. You descend quickly then, bearing left, begin to climb, crossing a **wooden bridge** and then steeply up to the stone steps to the **viewing platform** at **Phyllis Park** on the right. There are good views of Haro Strait, the San Juan Islands and, on a clear day, Mount Baker.

From the Phyllis Park viewpoint take the steps that lead down to **Arbutus Road**. Cross the road and take the footpath marked **Wedgepoint Park**. This short path winds through a grassy bold and Garry oaks before exiting on the roadway of **Wedgepoint Terrace**. Walk downhill turning left at the junction of the terrace and **Arbutus Road**. Walk 50 metres along Arbutus before taking a descending path through Arbutus Park on the left. (Because Arbutus Road circles the top of Ten Mile Point this path crosses the road twice. Don't be confused!)

The path crosses Arbutus Road and enters the trees. After 30 metres bear left at a fork in the path and descend to **Benson Road**. Continue down Benson a short distance to **Tudor Road**. Cross Tudor and descend the path down to **Seaview Road**. Turn right on Seaview and retrace the route back to the beach and carpark at Gyro Park. ●

TEN MILE POINT

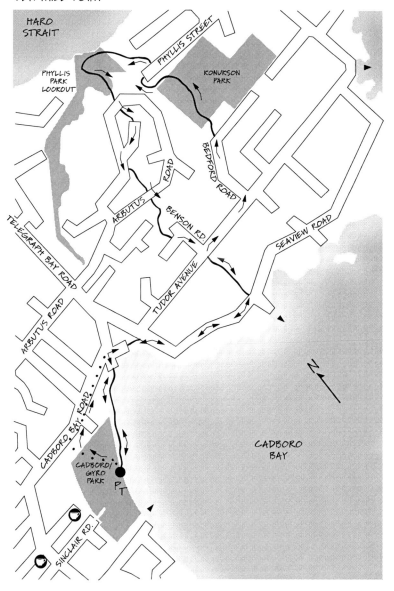

Colwood and Langford

26 FLORENCE LAKE/MILLSTREAM CREEK

Over the past decade the municipality of Langford has developed a network of trails throughout its district. These trails exist in natural settings and as gravelled roadside pathways. The walk I've designed is essentially a combination and a connecting of two such trails — the Strachan and Goldie Trails. The Strachan Trail primarily borders Florence Lake. It is named after Pat and Jean Strachan who were long time residents of the Florence Lake area. The Goldie Trail begins at Ida-Ann Lake and then connects the two ends of Goldie Avenue — a street divided in two by the course of Millstream Creek and a densely wooded area. The trail ends at the local elementary school.

General description
A suburban walk that embraces the different habitats of Florence Lake and Millstream Creek.

Location
Twelve kilometres west of downtown Victoria in the municipality of Langford.

Level Easy

Length 2 hours

Special attraction
Florence Lake viewing platforms; wooded trail along the banks of Millstream Creek; refreshments at Log House Pub.

How to get there
Follow Douglas Street out of town where it becomes the Trans-Canada Highway. Continue for about 10 kilometres. Shortly after the Millstream Road exit is the Spencer Road traffic light. Take the first right after Spencer Road on Savory Road. The

trailhead is about 200 metres on the right of Savory Road. Parking is permitted on the roadside. *(Bus # 57 Phelps.)*

THE WALK From the **Savory Road** trailhead descend down a gravel path for 20 metres onto a long **boardwalk** that passes over the south end of **Florence Lake**. The boardwalk has a wide viewing platform at its east end situated just before it terminates on **Brock Road**. The trail continues as part of the sidewalk of Brock. Just before Brock becomes **Florence Lake Road** the trail turns left for 30 metres effectively cutting the sharp corner of the junction of the two roads. The trail then joins Florence Lake Road and becomes its wide and safe sidewalk.

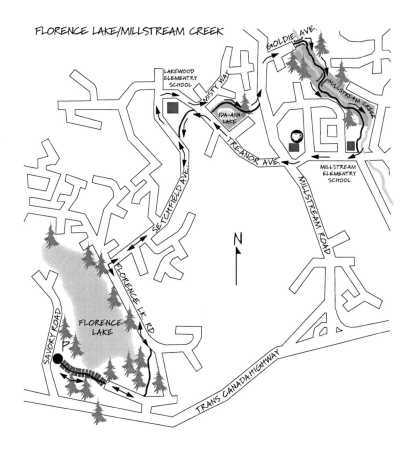

FLORENCE LAKE/MILLSTREAM CREEK

After 500 metres or so the trail moves closer to the lake a few metres parallel to the roadway. At the kilometre mark another **boardwalk** section begins comprising stairs down to the lake and a long bench. The trail crosses the road at this point at a pedestrian crossing and turning right begins a longish ascent up **Setchfield Road**. Keeping to the righthand gravel sidewalk trail follow Setchfield as it winds up toward **Skirt Mountain**.

After another kilometre the trail ends in front of **Lakewood Elementary School**. Continue past the school and a grassy banked play area on the narrow sidewalk for 50 metres until the intersection of Setchfield and **Treanor Avenue**. Turn right on Treanor and, after a short downhill section, cross to the left side of the road at the pedestrian crossing just past **Misty Way**.

Now take the trail that runs to the left of **Ida-Ann Lake**, a small lake built and maintained by the developers of the surrounding subdivision. At the lake's far end turn left on a paved cul-de-sac (**Ashley Road**) taking the short trail that leads to **Millstream Road**. At Millstream, cross over and turn left walking 30 metres before turning right on **Goldie Avenue**. The trail resumes at the bottom of this short road and enters a wooded area over a metal bridge spanning **Millstream Creek**. (This metal bridge is rumoured to have originally been a gangplank of a steamship running out of Victoria in the early 1900s.) It emerges onto the paved continuation of Goldie Avenue for a few metres and then re-enters the woods keeping a children's play area and picnic tables on the left.

Millstream Creek is soon crossed again, this time via a wooden bridge and the trail follows the creek upstream on its right bank. Ignore the access trail on the right about 50 metres past the bridge and continue along the trail as it swings left with the creek. Shortly after this bend is the **Millstream Elementary School** playground. This marks the end of the gravelled trail as it intersects Treanor Avenue.

Turn right on Treanor and, after two blocks, pass the **Log House Pub** on the right at the corner of Treanor and Millstream Road. Cross

Millstream at the light-controlled pedestrian crossing and walk up the long rise of Treanor as it curves to the right. Pass **Ida-Ann Lake** on the right and, almost directly opposite Misty Way, turn left up the entrance to **Lakewood Elementary School**. Walk around the school on its left side to joint Setchfield Avenue. Turn left on Setchfield and walk back to Florence Lake, the boardwalk and the trail back to Savory Road. •

· ·

27 LANGFORD LAKE/ED NIXON TRAIL

The municipality of Langford has won numerous awards for its innovative approach to community trail building. Walking the Ed Nixon Trail, you'll understand why.

Not far from the western shores of Langford Lake are the gravel pits owned and operated

Boardwalk on the Ed Nixon Trail

JAMES R. SMITH

by the Nixon family. And it's the patriarch Ed Nixon, the founder of the company whose name is given to the trail that partially circumnavigates the lake. The lake itself is almost two kilometres in length and is half a kilometre at its widest point. The municipality is dedicated to maintaining the lake as a healthy habitat for both fish and waterfowl and stocks the lake yearly with rainbow and cutthroat trout. Naturally, the lake has become a favourite fishing place for local residents and an ideal spot for bird watching plus a great place to walk.

General description

An out-and-back walk along the partially wooded western and southern shores of Langford Lake.

Location

Sixteen kilometres west of downtown Victoria off the Trans-Canada Highway.

Length

45 minutes to an hour out-and-back.

Level Easy

Special attractions

A viewing platform and a fishing pier built especially for anglers. In addition to rainbow and cutthroat trout, bass and perch are also fished. The lake's western extensive boardwalk is designed for wetland birding. Picnic sites.

How to get there

Take Douglas Street out of town where it becomes the Trans-Canada Highway. At the first set of traffic lights past the Millstream Road exit turn left at Spencer Road. Turn right on Goldstream Avenue. Travel along Goldstream for a kilometre or so and, on the left at the end of the lakefront housing, look for the Ed Nixon trailhead. There is a parking area on the right-hand side of Goldstream opposite the trailhead. *(Bus #58 Langford Meadows.)*

THE WALK From **Goldstream Avenue** the trail slopes south down a 20-metre stretch of gravel onto a short **boardwalk**. It continues to the right through a small clump of trees and then turns left over the western end of **Langford Lake's** wetland on a long, wide **boardwalk**. Halfway along this boardwalk is a viewing area with benches. As it leaves the boardwalk, the trail turns abruptly left and enters a stand of tall cedar and hemlock trees. Almost immediately there is a fork in the trail. Straight ahead is a **lakeside platform** and **picnic area**. The trail

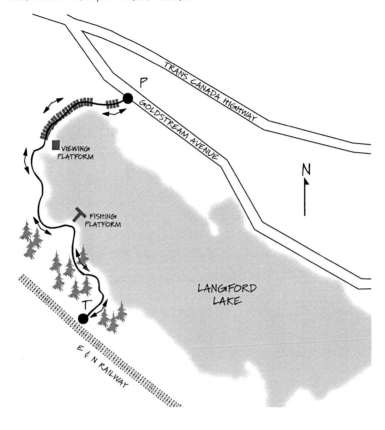

itself turns right at the fork and continues through the trees along the lake shore.

As the shoreline twists and winds, the trail traces a similar course through the woods trying to stay as close to the water as possible. There are glimpses of the lake's northern shore through the trees with **Skirt Mountain's** rocky and forested slopes a contrasting backdrop. For the next kilometre the trail is punctuated by short undulating stretches before unfortunately terminating just past a **fishing pier** and **picnic area** at a steep embankment to the **Esquimalt and Nanaimo Railway**. •

28 ROYAL ROADS UNIVERSITY (3 walks)

Established in the summer of 1995, Royal Roads University rose proverbially, from the ashes of a military college which had occupied the beautiful and extensive grounds of Hatley Park since 1940. The park is dominated by Hatley Castle which was built in 1909 by James Dunsmuir, a wealthy Scot who had made his money from coal and railways in the late 1800s and early 1900s. He commissioned the well-known Victoria architect Samuel Maclure to design what he hoped would be the ancestral home and two Boston landscape artists planned the grounds and garden. Dunsmuir's hope for a dynasty never materialized and,

JAMES R. SMITH

Skunk cabbage

in November of 1940, the federal government bought the estate for $75,000. The 228-hectare campus encompasses a variety of habitat including dense forest, open park land, a lagoon, a lake, formal gardens and a creek complete with gorge and waterfalls. Without doubt, there is nowhere in Victoria and its vicinity where such a variety exists within such close proximity.

General description

Three loop trails on varied terrain completely within the campus grounds of Royal Roads University. Mostly trail but some paved road.

Location

15 kilometres east of Victoria in the municipality of Colwood.

Length

Walk I: 2.5 hours
Walk II: 1 hour

Walk III: 30 minutes

Level Moderate

Special attractions

Creek-side trail with waterfalls; undulating trails through lush ever-green and mixed forest; historic Hatley Castle with its Italian and Japanese gardens; spectacular views of Esquimalt Lagoon, Juan de Fuca Strait and the Olympic Mountains.

How to get there

From downtown take Douglas Street out of town where it becomes the Trans-Canada Highway. After approximately 10 kilometres take the Colwood exit on the right passing underneath the Trans-Canada onto the Old Island Highway. Follow this busy road towards Sooke for three kilometres turning left into the main entrance to Royal Roads University/Hatley Park immediately after a pedestrian-crossing light. Parking lots are located about 400 metres down the main road — University Drive. (Bus #52 Wishart.)

WALK I From parking lots B or C walk toward the junction of **University Drive** (the main entrance to the university), **College Road** and **Cottonwood Creek Road**. On the left side of University Drive five metres before the junction turn sharply left on a marked trail down through the trees.

The trail follows **Cottonwood Creek** crossing it first at a small waterfall and again before the trail passes through a gully with stands of tall cedar, fir and alder trees. After 200 metres the trail turns left up a

flight of steps. Continue climbing left at the trail marker and follow a chain fence beyond which the creek flows through a picturesque **rocky gorge**. At the top of the climb the trail forks. Take the left fork away from the creek. There follows another set of steps after which the trail opens onto a meadow with a large **mock Tudor building** at the far left corner.

Although the trail disappears at this point, walk toward the large building taking a route to its left. Continue to the main entrance road, **University Drive**, and cross it walking 30 metres or so to the left. Turn right along the paved road that intersects here and walk 100 metres before taking the marked trail to the left opposite the **tennis courts**. The trail soon forks. Take the right fork following it as it winds through a flat wooded area and crosses a paved access road.

At the next fork turn right and then, at a four-way trail junction, continue straight ahead. The trail passes through a mixed forest with some giant cedars. Turn left at the next trail marker going down a steep decline then taking a sharp right at a **power pole**. The trail continues to descend for 100 metres or so before arriving at a narrow gravel road-way behind the **'Y' gym complex**.

If you want a shorter outing turn left at this gravel road walking down between the 'Y' buildings to the paved College Road at the bottom. Turn left on College Road and either:

WALK II Turn right off **College Road** directly opposite the 'Y' gym walking down **Cottonwood Creek Road** following it as it passes by the **Esquimalt Lagoon** and climbs back to the trail head and parking lots for a 1 hour walk.

WALK III Walk the kilometre and a quarter on **College Road** through the campus back to the trail head and parking lots for a 30 minute walk.

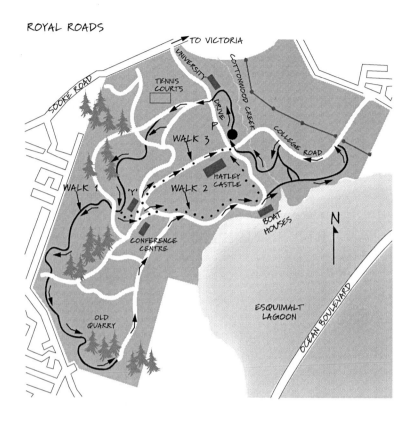

WALK I CONTINUED Turn right up this gravel road which soon intersects a paved road. Continue up this paved road for 30 metres taking the trail to the left climbing steeply for 75 metres. Turn left at the trail marker at the top and, after a further 50 metres turn right (ignoring the left pointing marker) along a wide gravel trail. This trail bends to the left through a broom-covered open area and terminates at the **gravel perimeter road** of the university grounds. Turn left on this perimeter road for a few metres before turning left then immediately right to follow a trail that runs through the woods parallel with the perimeter road. After half a kilometre the trail moves away from the perimeter road winding further into the woods. The trail soon crosses a wider trail and then turns sharply left on a well-established trail coming from the right. At the top of a steep rise the trail forks right about 15 metres before a little-used access road leading to an **abandoned gravel pit**. The trail then crosses the junction of two access roads to continue into the woods.

After a brief flat section the trail squeezes through two giant Douglas-fir trees and descends down a long, steep hill to join a gravel road. Turn left on this road and follow it as it descends further and then travels across an expanse of **marshy land** with an abundance of **alder trees**. After 400 metres a signed trail goes off to the left. Ignore it, continuing along the gravel road as it curves left through the trees.

Pass by the gate and, at the junction with the paved **Cottonwood Creek Road**, turn right and follow the paved road down towards the **Esquimalt Lagoon**. The road passes a small lake and the playing fields on the left and then, as it curves inland, the **boat houses** and pier on the right. Fifty metres past the boat houses, take the marked trail on the right which quickly drops down to **Cottonwood Creek** and crosses it

LAWRENCE McLAGAN

Rhododendron

over a wooden bridge. Over the bridge bear left up a short rise walking left around a small abandoned brick building. Turn right in front of the building and cross the **circular gravel road** taking the wide trail going to the right. After 200 metres or more the trail opens onto a high rocky outcropping — ideal for picnicking and taking in the superb views of the lagoon, the ocean and the Olympic Mountains.

The trail rises steadily turning left at a **pump house** and then left again along a high chain link fence. The trail ends at the paved **College Road** that heads into the campus from Belmont Road. Turn left and walk along this road for 400 metres. You then take a left turn down a gravel road opposite the 30 kph traffic sign walking some 300 metres before turning right down an unmarked side trail to the **remains of a bridge**.

Walk down to the creek side trail below and turn right to walk beside the creek. Cross the creek on a **wooden bridge** keeping to this left bank trail as it rises to the road above. Turn right on **Cottonwood Creek Road** and, walking over the four-way junction, arrive back at the trailhead and the parking lots beyond. •

. . . .

29 THETIS LAKE REGIONAL PARK (2 walks)

The First Nations certainly knew how to pick beautiful spots for their settlements and Thetis Lake Regional Park is an exquisite example of that. They hunted deer in the surrounding forest and brought clams from the bountiful beaches of nearby Esquimalt Harbour to lead, as we might imagine, a rather idyllic life. But with the establishment of Fort Victoria in 1842 things changed. Early white settlers were able to buy land in the area

— from Esquimalt Harbour to the southern part of the park. Then Thomas Harris, Victoria's first mayor, purchased more land until the city owned all the land included in the present park.

Along with Elk and Beaver Lake, Thetis Lake was for many years a major water supply for the city of Victoria. Present-day users of the park have to thank the Thetis Park Nature Sanctuary Association which, in 1957, was formed to preserve and protect the area from development. In 1993 the Capital Regional District took charge of the land and designated it a regional park.

The park's name derives from the British naval ship the HMS Thetis. The Thetis was a 36 gun sailing frigate which was commissioned, while stationed in Chile in 1852, to sail north to protect British rights as gold had been discovered on the west coast of the Queen Charlotte Islands.

General Description

Two loops in one of the area's most beautiful parks. The more rugged longer loop gives the walker a wilderness-like experience. The short loop is on a fairly groomed trail that circumnavigates both the upper and lower parts of Thetis Lake.

Location

Situated about 12 kilometres west of downtown Victoria off the Trans-Canada Highway.

Length

Long loop: 2 – 2.5 hours
Short loop: 1 hour

Level

Long loop: moderate to strenuous.
Short loop: easy to moderate.

Special attractions

Beautiful lake-side trail; extensive Douglas-fir and Garry oak forest. The more rugged long loop passes McKenzie Lake and follows McKenzie Creek for some distance. Beach and concession booth open in summer months.

How to get there

Take the Trans-Canada Highway out of town. After about ten kilometres take the Sooke/Colwood turn off. Turn right at the first set of lights onto Six Mile Road. Follow this road into the carpark of the park.
(Bus #50, 51, 52 and 61)

Overlooking Lower Thetis Lake

THE WALK: LONG LOOP From the **main carpark** take the marked **beach trail** at its left corner. Cross the paved fireroad turning left then right up to the beach. Walk between the **two beach buildings** turning left along the beach to take the path that meets the paved fireroad and drop-off area. Turn immediately right along the signed gravel trail to walk beside the lake. Pass through a parking lot at the end of a paved road climbing the short incline to a **trail junction**. Take the left trail which follows the lake's shoreline for almost a kilometre.

Ignore all trails to the left including the intriguing flight of wooden steps that lead to Phelps Road. Shortly after crossing the **bridge** over a seasonal creek follow the left trail away from a promontory to a trail junction with **McKenzie Creek Trail**. *(See below for a description of the short loop which begins here.) Take this narrow trail as it rises quickly to the left before dropping into a gully. It soon rises to the

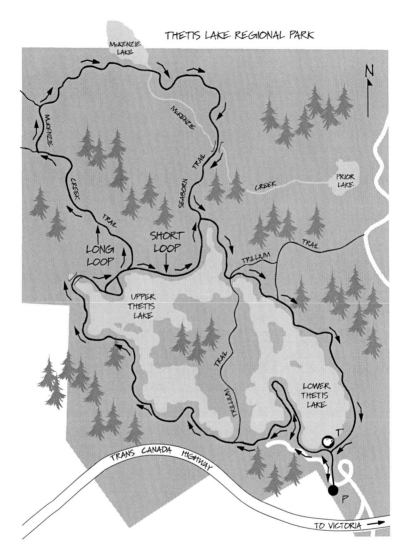

gully's right bank following it to pass another Phelps Trail marker.

At the next trail junction turn right to continue following the **McKenzie Creek Trail**. This trail now becomes very narrow, rocky and uneven — a veritable wilderness trail. Turn right again at another junction to follow the **Highland Road** direction of the trail. Two steeply-sided gullies now follow so be prepared for some grunt work. But the effort is worth it as **McKenzie Lake** comes into view through the trees on the trail's left side. You're now on your way back to Thetis Lake as the trail makes a long, meandering descent into some of the park's many wet areas. (This section has **plank bridges** and **log rounds** to make the way as dry as possible.)

At the beginning of a cedar and fern glade turn right over a **wooden bridge** up the signed **Seaborn Trail**. After a steady climb the trail becomes undulating before joining the main loop trail of the lake. Turn left here and again, keep the lake to your right. (This is the connection with the short loop.) The trail crosses the wide **Trillium Trail** and then a **wooden bridge** before rising abruptly up a series of **rough stone steps**. You then soon descend to the park's beach area and the loop's end.

THE WALK: SHORT LOOP Follow the trail described above until the junction with the McKenzie Creek Trail, marked *. At this point continue straight following the good trail as it hugs the shore. After a kilometre, at a sharp right turn in the trail, you'll meet the **Seaborn Trail** coming down from the left. (This is the junction with the Long loop.) Continue straight following the route described in the last two sentences of the above long loop. ●

Coastline Route:
From James Bay to Cordova Bay

As the name of this route implies, this series of nine walks follows the Victoria coastline from the Inner Harbour to the sweeping crescent of Cordova Bay, a distance of a little under 40 kilometres. Along the way you'll be introduced to some of Victoria's little known nooks and crannies.

Apart from the grand views of ocean, islands and mountains experienced at almost any point along the route, you'll be able to explore secluded beaches, sit on rocky promontories, walk down narrow, twisting tree-lined lanes, sip coffee overlooking a marina filled with rigging-slapping sail boats (on a windy day), and stroll through towering conifers on the edge of one of the areas largest parks.

For most of us, to do all nine walks of the route in one go would be quite a task (although it can be done), but one or two at a time going out and back in an hour or so is very "doable".

General description
A series of nine walks that follows the southern and eastern shores of the Victoria peninsula from the Inner Harbour to Cordova Bay. Mostly pavement with sections of path and beach walking.

Length
39 kilometres in total (See individual walks for times.)

Level Easy to moderate.

Special attractions
Each of the nine walks of this coastline route has its own list of attractions preceding the description of the walk.

How to get there
Because the walks in this section follow the continuous coastline of Victoria's peninsula and because a walker can choose any part of the route to begin a walk, I'm leaving how to get to the various departure points up to the reader and the use of a good Victoria street map.

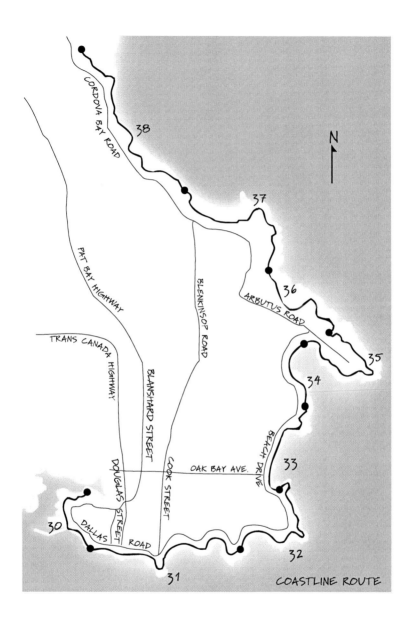

N

CORDOVA BAY ROAD

38

37

PAT BAY HIGHWAY

BLENKINSOP ROAD

ARBUTUS ROAD

36

35

TRANS CANADA HIGHWAY

BLANSHARD STREET

34

BEACH DRIVE

33

COOK STREET

OAK BAY AVE.

DOUGLAS STREET

30

DALLAS ROAD

32

31

COASTLINE ROUTE

111

30 INNER HARBOUR TO HOLLAND POINT

Length 45 minutes

Level Easy

Special attractions
Laurel Point Park; Fisherman's Wharf; Ogden Point breakwater and café.

THE WALK Walk west in front of the **Legislature Buildings** along **Belleville Street** keeping to the water side. Pass the Royal London Wax Museum, the Coho ferry terminal and the Victoria Clipper facility. Immediately after the entrance to the **Clipper parking lot** take a path

Houseboats at Fisherman's Wharf

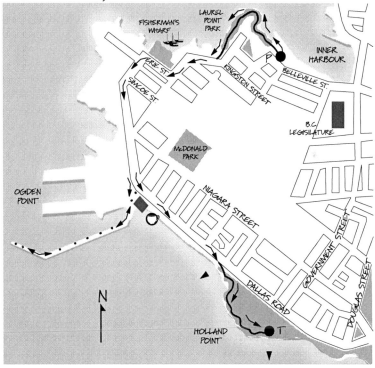

down to the right. This path goes to the water's edge then follows the shoreline to pass in front of the **Laurel Point Hotel** through Laurel Point Park. The path ends at the far side of the Coast Victoria Harbourside Hotel. Take the lane at the side of the hotel and turn right onto **Kingston Street**.

Follow Kingston a short distance until it becomes **St. Lawrence Street**. The entrance to **Fisherman's Wharf** is at this point. The wharf is an interesting collection of people and boats and is home to fishermen, house-boaters and sailors. One of Victoria's favourite fish and chips shop is located on the main dock. At the corner of an open playing field turn right on **Erie** walking for a block then turn left on **Dallas Road**.

The walk now passes by the Canadian Coast Guard docks and veers south and then east to **Ogden Point** where the Juan de Fuca Strait and the Olympic Mountains come into view. On a clear day, Mt. Olympus' snowy peak can be seen through the cleft in the closer mountains. Ogden Point is Victoria's port facility where merchant and cruise ships dock. You'll find a good interpretive display near the terminal building. It also serves as the helicopter terminal of Helijet Airways. At the head of the point's kilometre long breakwater is the **Ogden Point Café** — offering a great opportunity to rest and replenish, (especially if the walk out and back along the breakwater has been included). From the Point continue along the shoreline taking the cliff path onto the grassy **Holland Point**. •

. . . .

31 HOLLAND POINT (Beacon Hill Park) to KING GEORGE TERRACE LOOKOUT (Trafalgar Park)

Length 1 hour

Level Easy to moderate

Special attractions
Cliffside walk; Clover Point;

Ross Bay Cemetery where many of Victoria's rich and famous are buried; Gonzales Bay Beach; Chinese Cemetery; Trafalgar Park Lookout.

THE WALK From **Holland Point** continue to follow the cliff path as it joins the sidewalk of **Dallas Road**. At the junction of Dallas and Douglas follow the paved path along the cliff edge passing **Finlayson Point** and Horseshoe Bay before dropping gently down to **Clover Point**. You have a choice here of walking the perimeter of the point or taking the path across the grass to the pump house and the seawall.

COASTLINE ROUTE 31 – PART 1

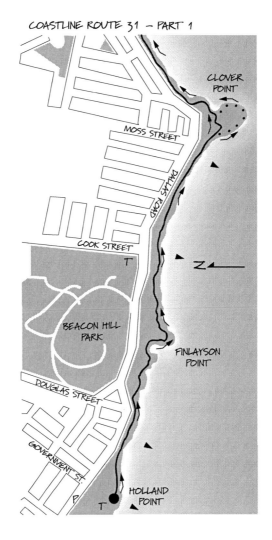

CLOVER POINT

MOSS STREET

DALLAS ROAD

COOK STREET

T

BEACON HILL PARK

FINLAYSON POINT

DOUGLAS STREET

GOVERNMENT ST.

HOLLAND POINT

T

COASTLINE ROUTE 31 - PART 2

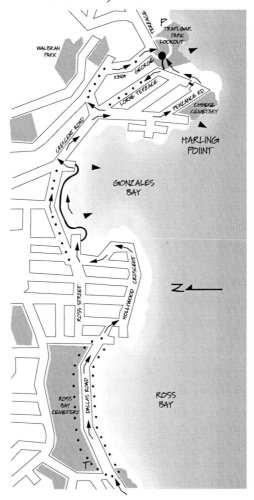

Either way, the seawall below Dallas Road is where the walk continues.

The seawall ends after about 400 metres and becomes the sidewalk of Dallas. Again, you have a choice: either continue along the sidewalk; walk the pebble beach to the stairs at the end of **Ross Bay** or cross the road and walk through the **Ross Bay Cemetery**. Whichever choice you make, continue, at the top of Dallas Road, along the right-curving sidewalk of **Hollywood Crescent**. This street soon intersects **Ross Street** at which point you turn sharply right walking 20 metres before dropping down through a tiny park onto **Gonzales Bay beach**.

Follow the beach to the left and, after about 200 metres at the end of the beach, exit up the concrete stairs to emerge onto **Foul Bay Road**'s dead end. (If the tide is unsuitable for walking the beach take **Crescent Road** which runs parallel to the beach.) Walk the few metres up Foul Bay Road turning right onto Crescent Road. Continue on Crescent following it as it turns right and descends down to the ocean and Harling Point.

At the bottom of Crescent on the left is the **Chinese Cemetery** — a wedge-shaped piece of land sandwiched between **Penzance Road** and **Crescent**. Visitors are welcome to walk in this historic cemetery. At the entrance to the cemetery is a plaque that describes why the land was chosen and the history of the burial ground.

Continue by walking along Penzance to its end where you'll turn left through a short open walkway to **Maquinna Street**. Walk straight ahead passing Quimper Street on the left and, as Maquinna joins **Lorne Terrace**, turn right and climb the 25-metre steep trail through **Trafalgar Park** to **King George Terrace** at the lookout at the top. (If you're unsure of attempting this short but steep climb, you can turn left and walk Lorne Terrace back to Crescent Road. Turn right at Crescent and climb King George Terrace to the lookout.) The lookout is a favourite spot offering panoramic view of the Olympic Mountains, the San Juan Islands and the Strait of Juan de Fuca. To the left and slightly off shore is Trial Island. •

Taking in the view from Oak Bay Marina

32 KING GEORGE TERRACE LOOKOUT TO OAK BAY MARINA

Length 45 minutes

Level Easy

Special attractions
Secluded beach; The Sloan Tree;
Oak Bay Beach Hotel; Turkey Head;
Oak Bay Marina restaurant and café.

THE WALK From King George Terrace's **Trafalgar Park Lookout** continue down the steep hill turning right to walk along **Beach Drive** as it follows the gentle curve of **McNeill Bay**. At the end of the bay the road bends left and begins to climb. On the right is **Hood Lane** which leads to **Radcliffe Lane**. Radcliffe dead-ends at a beach access and although the beach is small and pebbly it provides a pleasant spot to pause.

Beach Drive continues to rise as it slices through the beautiful **Victoria Golf Course**. On the left, just before the golf course entrance is the magnificent, multi-limbed Garry oak tree known as **The Sloan**

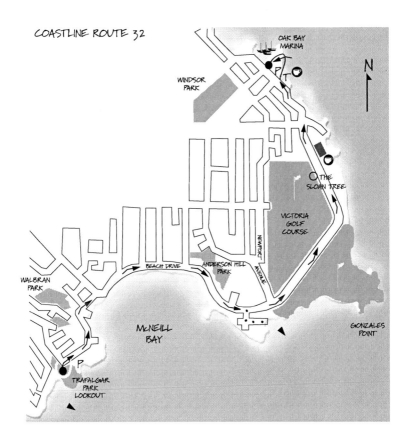

Tree. It was named in memory of the prominent Oak Bay resident Gordon Sloan who died in January of 1959.

A short distance past The Sloan Tree on the right is the **Oak Bay Beach Hotel** with its tea-serving restaurant and English-style pub, The Snug. Thirty metres on, at the junction of Beach and Margate Avenue, is the mini-park, **Oak Bay Nature Plant Garden**. This park/garden was donated to the people of Oak Bay in 1937 by the late Ada Beaven.

The walk continues downhill to the **Oak Bay Marina**. Turn right onto the park that circles **Turkey Head**, the name of the piece of land on which the marina is located. It's here that the walk ends — preferably in the café of the Oak Bay Marina. •

33 OAK BAY MARINA TO CATTLE POINT

Length 40 minutes

Level Easy

JAMES R. SMITH

Special attractions

Oak Bay Marina café, restaurant and gift shop; Glenlyon-Norfolk School; Willows Beach and Park; tea house, Cattle Point and Uplands Park.

THE WALK Exit the **Oak Bay Marina** carpark turning right on **Beach Drive**. The sidewalk follows the bay as it curves to the right passing the newly dedicated **Queens' Park**. Then, past the small **Haynes Park**, is the **Glenlyon-Norfolk School,** famous for having been designed, built and lived in by Victoria's turn of the century renowned architect Francis Rattenbury. (Rattenbury's design legacy is seen in the Legislature Building, the Empress Hotel, Government House, the Oak Bay Beach Hotel and a number of larger homes in the Rockland area.)

After the school take the unnamed lane past **Somas Drive** (the first street past the school). At the end of the lane turn left on **Bowker Place** and then first right on **Bowker Avenue**. There are only a few metres before Bowker Avenue terminates at the **Willows Beach** seawall path. Turn left along the seawall and continue in front of the park (with its tea house) onto the sidewalk of **Esplanade**. At the end of

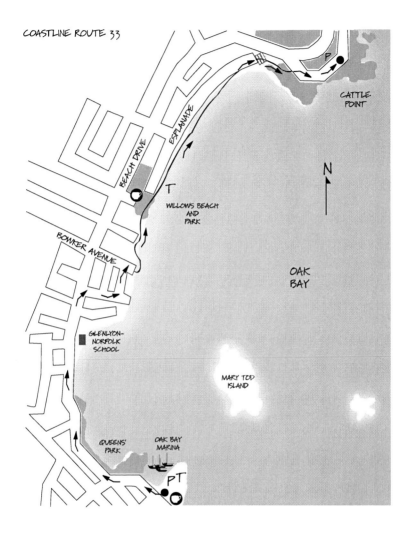

Esplanade climb the stairs up to **Cattle Point** where, after 50 metres or so, you'll find benches situated along the rocky shoreline. (For a more complete description of Willows Beach and Cattle Point see Walk 3.) •

34 CATTLE POINT TO CADBORO BAY/ GYRO PARK

Length 45 minutes

Level Easy

Special attractions
Uplands Park; Beach Drive as it
traverses the Uplands — an
exclusive suburb of Oak Bay; beach
accesses; Cadboro/Gyro Park and
beach; Cadboro Bay village with
stores and café.

THE WALK From the parking lot of **Cattle Point** walk east around
the one-way drive of the point. As the drive intersects **Beach Drive**
opposite the cenotaph turn right and, if you want to explore **Uplands
Park**, cross the road and enter the park on the path 20 metres right of
the **cenotaph**. There are no organized paths in the park, unfortunately,
but you can't get lost if you bear in mind that the ocean is on your left.
Whichever way is found, the Garry oaks, open meadows and low rocky
outcrops offer pleasant surrounds to the walk.

To walk directly to **Cadboro Bay** continue along **Beach Drive**
through the Uplands residential suburb characterized by large, stately
homes with gardens that, when visible, are intriguing and immaculate.
There are three beach accesses along the route; at the foot of
Rutland, at **Humber** and at the foot of **Lansdowne**. This latter is
through a grass and bush area between two houses onto Spoon Bay.
(The stone-capped gateposts of the first house is etched with the word
"**Riffington**", the name given to this, the first house ever to be built in
the Uplands.)

After the entrance to the **Royal Victoria Yacht Club**, Beach Drive
rises for 500 metres before passing through the stone pillars of the
Uplands gate. Beach now becomes **Cadboro Bay Road**. A few metres
on the right **Hibbens Close** descends toward the ocean. Take it and
walk to the bottom of the hill and down a flight of stairs to the beach.

COASTLINE ROUTE 34

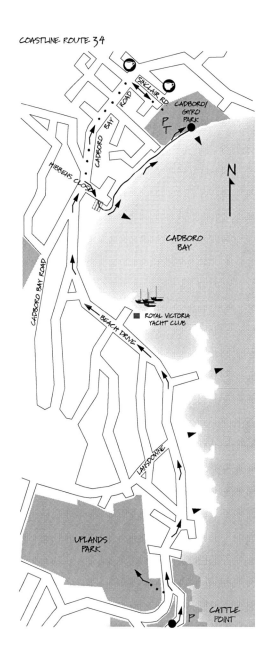

SINCLAIR RD

SINCLAIR ROAD

CADBORO BAY ROAD

CADBORO BAY

CADBORO GYRO PARK

P

HIBBENS CLOSE

N

CADBORO BAY

BEACH DRIVE

ROYAL VICTORIA YACHT CLUB

LANSDOWNE

UPLANDS PARK

CATTLE POINT

P

Turn left on the beach and walk the 200 metres to **Cadboro/Gyro Park**. (If the tide is too high to traverse the beach, walk down Cadboro Bay Road to Sinclair Road and turn right walking to the park.) •

• •

35 CADBORO BAY/GYRO PARK TO TEN MILE POINT

Length 1 hour

Level Easy to moderate

Special attractions
Quiet, countryside-type roads; many beach accesses (for views and picnics); Phyllis Park Lookout; Ten Mile Point is one of Victoria's most exclusive pieces of real estate. (For a more complete description and an alternate route for Ten Mile Point see Walk 25.)

THE WALK From **Cadboro/Gyro Park** walk east along the beach toward the bluffs of **Ten Mile Point**. About fifty metres before the bluffs, exit the beach onto the roadway and turn immediately right up the path of the no-exit **Tudor Avenue**. (If the tide is too high and the beach impassable take the footpath to the left (if you're facing the ocean) of the park toilets and walk to Cadboro Bay Road. Turn right here and walk the short distance to the steep path of Tudor Avenue just mentioned.) Turn right as the path joins the road taking **Seaview Road** as it descends to the right. This road twists and turns as it follows the shoreline of **Ten Mile Point**.

Seaview terminates at Tudor after a sharp left bend. Turn right on Tudor which quickly turns left and rises gently for 100 metres. At the top of the rise turn right along the tree-lined **McAnally Road**. McAnally turns left to become **Smuggler's Cove Road**. After a 100 metres or so Smuggler's Cove intersects **Baynes Road**. Turn right on Baynes and then left on **White Rock Street**. Just before the beach

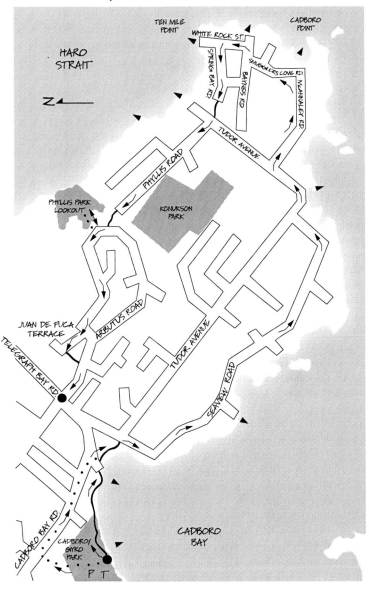

access turn left on **Spring Bay Road** walking up this short road to its dead-end where you'll find a trail leading to **Tudor Avenue**.

Turn left onto Tudor and then right onto the long steep hill of **Phyllis Street** passing through the fire gates at the top of the road. Turn right 15 metres after the gate onto **Arbutus Road**. Arbutus circles the top of Ten Mile Point and **Phyllis Park Lookout**, 50 metres on the right, offers great views to the east of Haro Strait, San Juan Island and Mt. Baker.

Descend Arbutus as it bears left and then take **Juan de Fuca Terrace** walking on its left side for about 60 metres to take a short trail leading down to Arbutus. Turn right and walk down this steep section of Arbutus to its junction with **Cadboro Bay** and **Telegraph Bay Roads**. •

Looking across Haro Strait from Phyllis Park Lookout

36 TEN MILE POINT TO GORDON HEAD VIA QUEENSWOOD

Length 45 minutes – 1 hour

Level Easy to moderate

Special attraction

Queenswood Drive; Goward House art exhibition (when happening); Hollydene Park; beach walking on Arbutus Cove beach; beach accesses.

THE WALK Turn right on **Telegraph Bay Road**, and after 200 metres turn left on **Queenswood Drive**. This tree-lined (lots of arbutus), narrow, twisting and hilly road is a delight to walk and, like so many roads in this neck of the woods, harbours some of Victoria's largest homes and gardens. There are three beach accesses along this stretch: at the bottom of **Telegraph Bay Road**, on **Crawford Place** and the other, on **Guinevere Place,** is ideal for sunrise watching.

Queenswood is more or less a large crescent and ends by joining **Arbutus Road**. Turn right on Arbutus passing **Goward House**, a senior's centre, on your left and the **G.R. Pearkes Clinic** and **Queen Alexandra Hospital** on your right. Just past the hospital Arbutus turns right after its junction with **Finnerty Road**. Follow Arbutus for 30 metres past Finnerty turning right down the no-exit **Locarno Lane**.

Locarno descends toward the point between **Finnerty** and **Arbutus Coves**. Just before the lane ends take the clearly visible

Descending onto Arbutus Cove

127

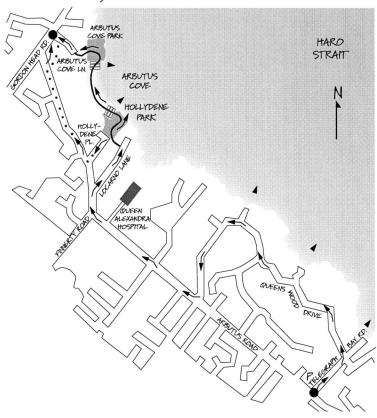

chip trail up to the left. After 50 metres turn sharply right on Hollydene Place and enter **Hollydene Park** down a good chip trail. This short trail ends abruptly above a rocky point. To the left and just before the point is a flight of wooden stairs leading down to the beach of **Arbutus Cove**. If the tide is favourable you can walk the 150-metre crescent to the flight of stairs leading up to **Arbutus Cove Park**. Turn left at the top of the stairs taking the paved path alongside **Arbutus Cove Lane** up to **Gordon Head Road**. (If the tide is too high to walk the beach, walk up Hollydene Place to Arbutus Road. Fifty odd metres before Arbutus joins Gordon Head Road, take the signed trail to the right. This will take you to Arbutus Cove Lane. Turn left to join Gordon Head Road.) •

37 ARBUTUS COVE LANE TO MOUNT DOUG PARK

Length 1.25 hours

Level Easy to moderate

Special attraction
Rocky shores of Glencoe Cove/Kwatseck Park; Vantreight Park; some delightful back streets of the Gordon Head suburb.

THE WALK Turn right off **Arbutus Cove Lane** onto **Gordon Head Road** following it as it swoops left to become **Ferndale Road**. As you pass James Houlihan Park on your left you immediately turn right down the rather unobtrusive **Evergreen Place**. This short lane connects with **Shore Way** by a protected fire lane. Turn left on Shore Way walking to its end and enter **Glencoe Cove/Kwatseck Park** on the right. Follow the trail to the left as it traces the rocky shoreline of **Gordon Point**. (This is a gem of an ocean-front park and is a great place for mid-afternoon picnics.)

Arbutus leaves

COASTLINE ROUTE 37

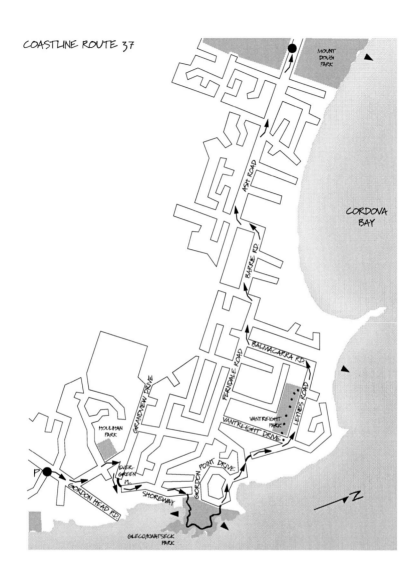

MOUNT
DOUG
PARK

CORDOVA
BAY

ASH ROAD

BARRE RD

BALMACARRA RD

FERNDALE ROAD

LEYNES ROAD

VANTREIGHT
PARK

VANTREIGHT DRIVE

GRANDVIEW DRIVE

HOULIHAN
PARK

GORDON POINT DRIVE

EVER-
GREEN
PL.

SHOREWAY

GORDON HEAD RD.

P

N

GLECOJONATSECK
PARK

Exit the park after about 100 metres or so as the trail turns left to meet the roadway of **Gordon Point Drive**. Turn right on the road walking another 100 or so metres before taking a gravel path on the right. This soon joins **Leynes Road**, a shady lane with woods on the left and large gardens on the right. Continue on Leynes Road as it crosses **Vantreight Drive** or walk through **Vantreight Park** just to the left and running parallel with Leynes Road. Either way, turn left on **Balmacarra Road** (there's a beach access to the right) and walk up this steep hill to turn right on **Ferndale Road**.

You follow Ferndale up the hill and, after the road bears left take the first right onto **Barrie Road**. Barrie ends at **Ash Road** at which point you turn right on Ash and descend the long hill toward **Mt. Doug Park**. •

. . . .

38 MOUNT DOUG PARK TO MATTICK'S FARM

Length 1.5 hours

Level Easy

Special attraction
Mt. Doug's shoreline park; tall

Douglas-fir; long beach walk on Cordova Bay; McMorran's Beach House Restaurant and Café; shops, café and farmer's market at Mattick's Farm.

THE WALK As **Ash Road** flattens and curves to the right to junction with **Cordova Bay Road** you'll notice, on the right, a large sign announcing **Mount Douglas Park**. Shortly after the sign and after crossing Douglas Creek take the trail marked "**Beach**". This trail follows the steep-sided gully of the creek for almost two hundred metres before it forks. If you want to visit the beach and the **creek's estuary**, bear right following the direction of the gully.

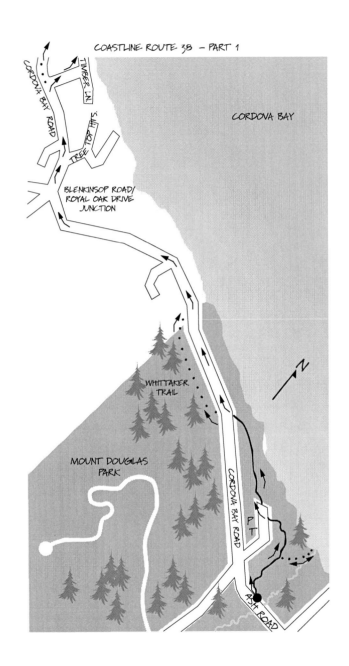

COASTLINE ROUTE 3B — PART 1

CORDOVA BAY

CORDOVA BAY ROAD

TIMBER LN.

TREE TOP S.R.

BLENKINSOP ROAD/
ROYAL OAK DRIVE
JUNCTION

WHITTAKER
TRAIL

MOUNT DOUGLAS
PARK

CORDOVA BAY ROAD

P
T

ASH ROAD

N

COASTLINE ROUTE 38 - PART 2

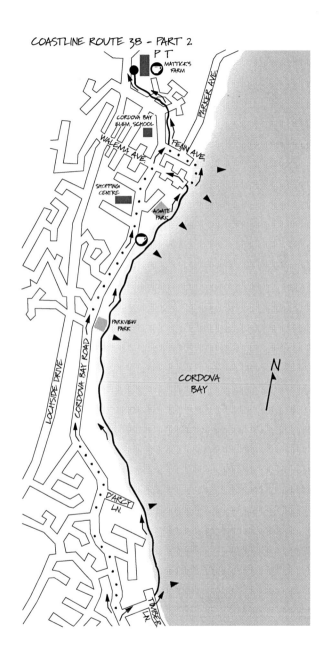

PT

MATTICK'S FARM

CORDOVA BAY ELEM. SCHOOL

PARKER AVE.

FENN AVE.

WALEMA AVE.

SHOPPING CENTRE

AGATE PARK

PARKVIEW PARK

LOCHSIDE DRIVE

CORDOVA BAY ROAD

CORDOVA BAY

N

D'ARCY LN.

TIMBER LN.

To continue the walk, pass through the picnic area and exit the parking lot at its far north end on the paved trail up to its meeting with **Cordova Bay Road**. You can either turn right on Cordova Bay Road walking the kilometre to its junction with **Blenkinsop Road** and **Royal Oak Drive** or cross Cordova Bay Road and re-enter the park on the **Whittaker Trail**. Turn right on the trail walking roughly parallel to the road and, at the trail's end, walk down to the road, continuing up to the Blenkinsop/Royal Oak Drive junction. (Take care on this stretch of road as there is little sidewalk to speak of.)

At the junction follow **Cordova Bay Road** as it turns right. Within 400 metres you'll come to the first of several beach accesses along the bay, **Timber Lane**. Walk up the lane on its left side and, as it intersects **Timber Place**, cross over bearing left to find the beach access trail between two large houses. A long flight of stairs leads down to the beach. From this point, if the tide is right, you're able to continue the walk on this gravel and sand beach. (If it's not possible to walk the beach follow Cordova Bay Road and, if you like, poke your nose into the beach accesses along the way.)

There are ample escape routes along the way of course, via the access stairs — identified by their metal rails and concrete steps — or the three mini-parks of **Parkview**, **Agate** and **McMorran** — this latter being beside **McMorran's restaurant and patio**. The last possible way back up to Cordova Bay Road is the flight of stairs at the end of **Fenn**, but my suggestion is to exit through the flatter access of **Walema Avenue** just before Fenn. Walk up Walema to join Cordova Bay Road and turn right. Soon you'll notice a paved walkway that runs parallel to the road. Take this path until the route's end at **Mattick's Farm**. •

RECORD OF YOUR WALKS

Name of Walk	Date	Comments
. . . .	. . . .	. . . .
. . . .	. . . .	. . . .
. . . .	. . . .	. . . .
. . . .	. . . .	. . . .
. . . .	. . . .	. . . .
. . . .	. . . .	. . . .
. . . .	. . . .	. . . .
. . . .	. . . .	. . . .
. . . .	. . . .	. . . .
. . . .	. . . .	. . . .
. . . .	. . . .	. . . .
. . . .	. . . .	. . . .
. . . .	. . . .	. . . .
. . . .	. . . .	. . . .
. . . .	. . . .	. . . .
. . . .	. . . .	. . . .
. . . .	. . . .	. . . .
. . . .	. . . .	. . . .
. . . .	. . . .	. . . .
. . . .	. . . .	. . . .
. . . .	. . . .	. . . .
. . . .	. . . .	. . . .
. . . .	. . . .	. . . .
. . . .	. . . .	. . . .
. . . .	. . . .	. . . .

RECORD OF YOUR WALKS

Name of Walk	Date	Comments
. . . .	. . . .	. . . .
. . . .	. . . .	. . . .
. . . .	. . . .	. . . .
. . . .	. . . .	. . . .
. . . .	. . . .	. . . .
. . . .	. . . .	. . . .
. . . .	. . . .	. . . .
. . . .	. . . .	. . . .
. . . .	. . . .	. . . .
. . . .	. . . .	. . . .
. . . .	. . . .	. . . .
. . . .	. . . .	. . . .
. . . .	. . . .	. . . .
. . . .	. . . .	. . . .
. . . .	. . . .	. . . .
. . . .	. . . .	. . . .
. . . .	. . . .	. . . .
. . . .	. . . .	. . . .
. . . .	. . . .	. . . .
. . . .	. . . .	. . . .
. . . .	. . . .	. . . .
. . . .	. . . .	. . . .
. . . .	. . . .	. . . .

Adapting this book to be more user-friendly

You've noticed, I'm sure, that when a paperback gets a lot of use the spine slowly disintegrates and pages start to fall out. This is especially true of guidebooks when they are constantly being referred to on a walk or hike.

A trick I learned many years ago was that as soon as I bought a guidebook, I'd take it to my favourite photocopying store and have them spiral bind the thing. It works like a charm. You open the guide at the selected page and fold it over. The pages are individually kept in place by the plastic spiral not the glue. This way the book will last forever — almost.